WHERE IS GOD NOW?

Nuclear Terror, Feminism, and the Search for God

Juliana M. Casey, I.H.M.

Sheed & Ward

IN MEMORY OF MY MOTHER

MARGUERITE HOURIGAN CASEY

AND IN CELEBRATION OF MY SISTERS

NANCY CASEY NORTON

PATRICIA CASEY REED

Wonderful women

whose goodness, courage, and laughter

have taught me more

of where God is

than any book or study

Sheed & Ward™ is a service of National Catholic Reporter Publishing, Inc.

Library of Congress Catalog Card Number: 86-63341

ISBN: 1-55612-053-2

Published by: Sheed & Ward
115 E. Armour Blvd. P.O. Box 414292
Kansas City, MO 64141-0281

To order, call: (800) 821-7926

CONTENTS

PREFACE

Over five years ago, I received a telephone call from Sr. Lora Ann Quinoñez, C.D.P., who was then the Executive Director of the Leadership Conference of Women Religious. Lora Ann asked if I would be willing to serve as the L.C.W.R.'s representative on the Bishops' committee charged with writing a pastoral letter on war and peace. I would have to attend "a few" meetings, she said; and no, I did not have to be an expert on nuclear weapons.

I agreed, and my life changed. The "few" meetings became several dozen meetings, many lasting for two days or more. My knowledge of nuclear weapons grew tremendously, as did my fear of their use. I met many people I would otherwise have never known. Some of these people were famous, some were not. Some of them inspired me, others terrified me. The pastoral letter, which went through three revisions, became a source of news for the media, controversy for many people, hope for some. Many times in the almost two years of the committee's life I experienced that rare sense of being part of history; more often, however, I felt only the difficulties, the frustrations, and the genuine worries of both of those who set our nation's policies and those who want to change those policies. Everyone who served on that committee genuinely *served*. They gave enormous amounts of their time and energy; they summoned up wisdom and courage from places deep inside themselves; they assumed the burden of controversy and the even greater burden of entering into the terrible world of nuclear weapons.

My own experience on the committee was unique. I was the only woman. I sometimes felt very lonely; not because I was ig-

iv

nored or devalued, but because I knew my perspectives were different, my contexts other than those of everyone else. My own consciousness of this led me to realize the tragic absence of the feminine in the most vital of our country's and our church's spheres in new and intensified ways.

Service on that committee took me to places I had never gone and taught me things I would rather not have learned. More importantly, it took me to places inside myself that had remained unknown to me, and it gave me insights I would not have dared hope for. Even as I spent sleepless nights trying to forget the awful facts I had learned, or wrestled with nightmares of nuclear holocaust, even then I realized that God's Spirit was involved in this work, that God whispered hope and grace in the midst of terror.

During those years, the questions I asked gradually changed. At first they were questions about how a committee can write a pastoral letter, or about what certain words and acronyms meant. Later, I began to ask how we had reached this terrible impasse; what is it that keeps us there? Ultimately, I asked the real question: Where is God in all of this?

Any answers to these questions were profoundly influenced by three other aspects of my life. As a woman religious in the U.S. in these times, I have inevitably come to the realization of the importance of the women's movement and of the valuable insights offered in recent feminist writings. As a person who has studied and taught scripture, my questions always lead me to the Word and its inexhaustible mystery. Thus, peacemaking became inextricably connected to feminism and to scriptural paradigms. As a believer, graced with hunger for the God who is with us, the struggle to learn to make peace could lead to no other place than to God.

What I offer in this book is not the final word on any of these issues, to any of the myriad questions. It is, rather, an offering of my own journey, of the insights I have gleaned from many sources. I begin (as *I* began) with some basic facts about the "growth and development" of these terrible weapons. I then look to the costs of nuclear weapons — costs to the society and to the psyche. Chapter Three explores patterns and modes of behavior which encourage violence and endanger our lives, while Chapter Four looks to the alternatives which feminist consciousness offers us. Chapters Five and Six turn (as *I* turned) to God's Word and God's presence. Hopefully there is hope in this book and some slight glimpse of God's caring presence in our midst.

I have come to know that presence in many ways since the day of that phone call, and I celebrate in gratitude the persons who have shown me the divine among us. I have found myself constantly amazed and encouraged by the continued dedication of so many people: those who would take time to attend a lecture after a busy day; those who would create ribbons and write peaceful songs; those who would travel and march and sit down for peace; those who would dare to examine their own lives; those, finally, who would pray. To all of you, I say *Shalom.*

I am immeasurably grateful to the marvelous women of my own religious congregation, The Sisters, Servants of the Immaculate Heart of Mary (Monroe, Michigan), and most especially those of the Northeast Province whose support was constant and gracious. They were a blessing to come home to, and constant witness of the gospel for me. Two of them, Sisters Jeannette Walters and Fran Mlocek, provided gracious hospitality, sensitive listening, and wondrous diversion whenever I was in Washington for committee meetings. They were my lifeline to hope many, many times.

Many people have encouraged me in the writing, and so empowered me in the doing. They have been gift to me, and I thank them, especially Dr. Nadean Bishop whose insight and expertise have enriched this work. I am grateful to the I.H.M. Sisters for a sabbatical year in which to write, and to my father whose love for peace and nature led him long ago to provide a beautiful place in which to write.

And I am grateful for the phone call.

1
"I Do Not Want to See It"
NUCLEAR FACTS

In their 1983 Pastoral letter, *The Challenge of Peace: God's Promise and Our Response,* the U.S. Catholic Bishops state: "Peacemaking is not an optional commitment. It is a require-ment of our faith."[1] If taken seriously, this statement is undoubtedly the most radical one in a very controversial docu-ment. It demands an active involvement in the difficult task of peacemaking and grounds that involvement in our faith itself. If we believe, the Pastoral says, we must be peacemakers. With this declaration the struggle for peace is removed from the periphery of Christian life and is placed where it belongs — at its very center. Here the "Challenge of Peace" becomes very real and very demanding for all of us.

The Bishops' statement inevitably raises questions which are not easily answered. What does it mean to be a peacemaker in the nuclear age, and why is it a requirement of *faith*? There are many ways of making peace and multiple reasons for doing so. One can make a certain peace by silencing opposition or over-coming enemies. One can desire peace for the sake of order or for economic gain. Faith-filled peacemaking is something more and other than this, however, and the peace it seeks is found not in negotiations or superior strength, but rather in the very heart of God.

1

Faith-filled peacemaking is a never-ending process which involves the whole person. It demands that we use our minds in order to learn the facts of the nuclear reality and our bodies to act to change the impossible situation in which we find ourselves. This process also calls us to look to our own consciences and the collective conscience of our country, to be willing to see there that which enslaves us, to search for alternatives, and to come to the courage of conversion. Faith-filled peacemaking will lead us to the sources of our faith, to the Word of God and eventually to encounter with God.

This process is a difficult one particularly because much of what we learn is frightening, and much of what we must face is menacing. To struggle for peace is to learn a great deal about war and weapons and the mentalities and values which make for war. It is to acknowledge our own participation in these mentalities, to confront our own sinfulness. We begin to sense the nonsense of the nuclear age and, at times, the absence of our God. But God is often present in felt absence, nonsense must be named, and the facts must be gathered for the making of peace.

This first chapter is an attempt to gather some of the more salient facts about the present nuclear menace. Anyone familiar with the vast amount of literature concerning nuclear weapons and the arms race will recognize that what is here presented remains an incomplete picture of all that is involved; yet we must begin somewhere. Most who read this chapter will share in a distaste and dis-ease with the numbers and descriptions and costs of nuclear weapons. Many will resonate with the words of Dorothee Soelle.

> . . . I was reading during the last four months, during the last fall and winter, a lot of peace research, and a terrible thing happened to me, namely that I couldn't keep this in my mind, the numbers just fell away, just dropped out of my head, and I couldn't get it into a serious theoretical understanding. I felt all

the time misled, my good faith in science was misused, I felt confused . . .[2]

When Soelle uses these words to describe her experience, she gives voice to a very common phenomenon. Most of us can remember all sorts of numbers and numerical combinations. We know phone numbers, zip codes, lock combinations and social security numbers, but when it comes to megatons, the number of missiles in existence, or the estimated numbers of casualties expected in a nuclear exchange, our minds go blank. We can't remember a thing. One of the reasons for this phenomenon is the often conflicting numbers we read or hear; another is the sheer enormity of these numbers when one talks about military budgets or nuclear casualties. There are deeper reasons, however, for our seeming inability to "get it into a serious theoretical understanding." Soelle speaks of fear.

I was so afraid to realize what is going on, to think about it in clear consequences, that I couldn't keep it in my mind, my mind couldn't really function in the way it otherwise would function, because I do not want to see it and I do not want to hear it.[3]

We are afraid, we don't want to see, we don't want to hear. The Gospel of John tells us that "the truth will make you free" (Jn 8:32). Our teachers always told us that learning was fun (even though most students remained unconvinced!), and conventional wisdom declares that knowledge is power. Learning about nuclear weapons is not fun, though, and knowledge about the nuclear reality does not make us feel very powerful. The truth about ICBMs, MX missiles, defense budgets, MAD, and counter value targeting overwhelms and paralyzes us before it makes us free. The facts terrorize us, numb us, lead us to a never really effective forgetfulness. If we would have any say in our future and in the future of this earth which is our home, however, it is absolutely necessary for us to come to grips with at least a basic understanding of the concrete reality of the world

of nuclear weapons — their present and potential significance.
What follows is a brief introduction to that which many of us do
not want to see or to hear.

History and Development

In January, 1939, Nobel Prize physicist Niels Bohr brought
the news of research in nuclear fission being done by German
scientists to the United States.[4] Fearful that such research
would lead to the development of an atomic weapon on the the
part of the Germans, scientists in the U. S. attempted to enlist
the interest and concern of American military officials. When
their efforts were unsuccessful, they sought to approach the
President. On October 11, 1939, Alexander Sachs met with
President Roosevelt and delivered a letter to him from Albert
Einstein. Einstein's letter urged the President to take seriously
the new scientific developments and to see that funds were provided which would enable the U. S. scientists to speed up their
research. Roosevelt agreed to do so.

Intensive research and experimentation ensued at Oak
Ridge, Tenn., Berkeley, Calif., Princeton, N.J. and Chicago. In
1942, the various projects were brought together under the
name of the Manhattan Project. This project was eventually
housed in Los Alamos, New Mexico, in 1943. On July 16, 1945,
an experimental plutonium bomb, code-named Trinity, was
exploded near Alamogordo, New Mexico. On August 6, 1945, a
uranium bomb ("Little Boy") was dropped on Hiroshima, Japan.
On August 9, 1945, a plutonium bomb ("Fat Man") was dropped
on Nagasaki, Japan. The Hiroshima bomb was ten feet in
length, weighed 9,000 pounds, and yielded 20 kilotons of explosive power. The casualties in Hiroshima numbered between
130-150,000 persons by December, 1945. Delayed deaths increased that number to an estimated 200,000 by 1950. The
Nagasaki bomb, approximately the same size and weight, re-
sulted in only half as many casualties. The explosion was off
target.[5]

In 1945, two atomic weapons existed. Both were exploded and thus destroyed. The creation of these weapons was originally viewed in terms of defense, protection against German forces which might produce similar weapons. Their actual use, however, was as *offensive* weapons — against Japan. On August 10, 1945, after the bombing of Nagasaki, there were no atomic weapons. On August 10, 1985, only forty years later, there were approximately 50,000 nuclear weapons in existence. How did we get from there to here? Perhaps by a combination of scientific genius, determination to excel, increasing mistrust of other nations (particularly the Soviet Union), and a general loss of the sense of proportion and even of reality.

The Arms Race

After the end of World War II, the Soviet Union became involved in the production of atomic weapons. On August 29, 1949, the first Soviet atomic explosion took place in Siberia.[6] Soviet possession of atomic weapons, combined with other events such as the Berlin blockade, the invasion of Czechoslovakia in 1948, the fall of China to Mao-Zedong's troops in 1949, and the outbreak of the Korean conflict in 1950, contributed greatly to the development of the U. S. nuclear arsenal. On January 31, 1950, President Truman directed the Atomic Energy Commission to "continue its work on all forms of atomic weapons, including the so-called hydrogen or superbomb."[7] On May 8 and 24, 1951, the U. S. successfully exploded "George" and "Item," the first thermonuclear bombs. Atomic weapons had become nuclear weapons. Fission ("atoms of a heavy element — uranium or plutonium — change, or transmute, into lighter elements") had developed into fusion ("two light nuclei — certain isotopes of hydrogen or lithium — combine to form other nuclei").[8]

In November, 1952, "Mike" was exploded. This weapon was the "first true superbomb"[9] and was 1,000 times more powerful than those dropped on Hiroshima and Nagasaki. "Mike" yielded the equivalent of ten million tons of TNT. August 12, 1953, witnessed the first Soviet explosion involving thermonuclear reaction. In 1954, there were six explosions of superbombs by the United States. The largest of these, "Bravo," yielded fifteen megatons of explosive power. On November 23, 1955, the Soviet Union exploded *its* first true superbomb.

Experimentation and the building of weapons has been continuous since that time. The 1950s were marked by the manufacture of bombs to be carried by long-range bombers. The U.S. built faster jet bombers which enabled faster delivery of nuclear weapons. The Soviet Union, while it built some long-range bombbers, concentrated more on "large numbers of short-range, fast interceptor aircraft."[10] Both nations tested their first Intercontinental Ballistic Missiles (ICBM) in the late fifties.

The introduction of the ICBM was an important step in the arms race. Ballistic missiles travel in space orbit. They do not, therefore, need to burn large amounts of fuel, nor do they require planes to transport them. Further, they can be launched either from the ground, from planes, or from submarines. An intercontinental missile can "orbit full intercontinental distances within about thirty minutes."[11]

The sixties were marked by the establishment of the pattern of nuclear weapons which we have today: a "Triad," consisting of missile launchers on land, underwater, and in the air. The U. S. had developed a lead over the Soviet Union, particularly in numbers of ICBMs, but the Soviet Union eventually caught up in this area.[12] The U. S. also built up its submarine fleet during this time, and the Soviet Union has been at work increasing its submarine forces. The U. S., however, still maintains the advantage in submarine forces and in the number of intercontinental bombers.

In the seventies, the U. S. pursued a rapid buildup in the number of nuclear warheads. It did so primarily through a process of building multiple-warhead missiles such as the Multiple Re-entry Vehicles (MRV) and the Multiple Independently-targetable Re-entry Vehicles (MIRV). MRVs contain several small warheads instead of one large one. MIRVs contain separate warheads which can each be aimed at different targets. The latest development, Maneuverable Re-entry Vehicles (MARV), will also be able to maneuver to avoid a defensive weapon and still reach their targets accurately.[13]

Technological developments have not only made nuclear weapons more numerous and more easily launched, they have also made them more destructive. The first thermonuclear bomb was 1,000 times more powerful than the first atomic bombs. The 1970 Minuteman III (an ICBM) carries three warheads, each with 170 kilotons of explosive power. It can destroy over ten times the area of the Hiroshima bomb. The Missile Experimental (MX) will carry ten warheads of 350 kilotons each. *It* can destroy over fifty times the area of the Hiroshima bomb.

In 1983, President Reagan announced a new direction in arms systems: the Strategic Defensive Initiative (SDI — commonly and continuously called "Star Wars"). This system would employ several layers of weapons — based either in space or with their beams reflected off space-based mirrors — capable of intercepting and destroying Soviet ICBMs as they would travel through space toward their targets in the U.S.

The Star Wars plan is a radical departure from traditional strategies in at least two ways. In the first place, this plan would move the nuclear war battlefields into outer space, thus providing the possibility of a true war among the stars. Secondly, the SDI is a *defense* system whereas all other weapons systems have been offensive. The introduction of a comprehensive defense system is viewed by many as destabilizing. Deterrence has traditionally been based upon the offensive capabilities of each nation. Both have enough nuclear weapons to destroy an adversary; therefore, it would be foolhardy to begin a nuclear war. If one nation, however, has both offensive weapons *and* a system of defense, the other nation will feel itself threatened to such an extent as to at least intensify its own development of a similar system — if it does not strike first, before the SDI is in place.

Proliferation

In 1945, the U. S. was the only country to possess atomic weapons; the Soviet Union had them shortly after in 1949. Other nations have since joined what has often been called the "world's most exclusive club." Today, Great Britain, France and China are known to possess nuclear weapons. South Africa and Israel are viewed as having nuclear capability, and India carried out a nuclear explosive test in 1974.[14]W. M. Arkin and R. W. Fieldhouse offer an outline of the world nuclear arsenals in the 1985 work, *Nuclear Battlefields: Global Links in the Arms Race.*[15] The U.S. possesses approximately 26,000 nuclear warheads, the Soviet Union between 22,000 and 33,000; Britain has 686; France, 514; and China between 251 and 331.

Not only are there great numbers of nuclear weapons; they are also spread out all over the world. Within our own country, nuclear weapons are permanently stored in 28 states. Forty-one of the 50 states have some major nuclear force component (bomber bases, missile silos, submarine bases, command centers) within their borders. The U. S. maintains over 1,000 ICBMs which carry a total of 2,100 nuclear warheads. These ICBMs are presently housed in underground silos which are spread over ten states and cover an area of 80,000 square miles.

The U. S. also has nuclear weapons in other countries: Guam, Belgium, Greece, Italy, the Netherlands, Turkey, South Korea, the United Kingdom, and West Germany. In addition, there are about 1,400 warheads at sea in the Atlantic, Pacific and Indian Oceans and in the Mediterranean.

The Soviet Union, too, has apparently exported some of its weapons. Researchers strongly suspect that Czechoslovakia, East Germany, Hungary and Poland host Soviet nuclear weapons. In addition, there are four submarine bases, twenty airfields and five Arctic staging bases where Soviet bombers can land enroute to targets in the U. S.[16]

Britain's nuclear warheads, indeed its entire nuclear capability, is strongly allied with that of the U. S. One could use the word "intertwined" without exaggeration. France, on the other hand, maintains its own nuclear force, and all of its land-based weapons are on French soil. It also has three submarines which carry 48 nuclear missiles among them. China's weapons are thought to be aimed at Soviet targets.

Targeting

The procedures for establishing targets, assigning them priorities, and actually aiming weapons at these targets are complex, often convoluted, and constantly changing. A comprehensive statement concerning the U. S. targeting doctrine is contained in a document known as "Presidential Directive 59." This directive, which was leaked to the press in 1980, deals with 40,000 targets for approximately 9,200 nuclear warheads. One-half of these targets are Soviet military targets; 15,000 are economic and industrial, 2,000 are aimed at leadership centers, and an additional 3,000 are termed "counterforce opportunities."[17]

The use of the term "counterforce" is significant here. There are two major areas of targeting: counter*force,* which is an attack against the nuclear weapons and military forces of the enemy, and counter*value,* which is the destruction of enemy population centers and natural resources. U.S. spokespersons have maintained that the government's targeting doctrine is counterforce rather than countervalue. They always add, however, a proviso which is rather ominous: *"per se."* The problem becomes extremely difficult when a counterforce target happens to be in the middle of a countervalue area (a weapons plant within close proximity to a major city, for example).

The Soviet doctrine also eschews population centers as such.[18] But the same problems occur. The U.S. Federal Emergency Management Agency (FEMA), in an attempt to prepare for national emergencies in a nuclear conflict, has established a list of high risk areas within the U. S. This list contains 60 counterforce areas, 250 metropolitan areas, and 100 additional areas of "important military and economic installations." A map of the country with all of these potential targets indicated shows targets in every single state and several targets in many of them.[19]

In addition to the thousands of targets within the U.S. and the Soviet Union, one must also take into account the multiple targets in Europe, the Middle East, and the Pacific. There are few areas in our world which are not potential targets for nuclear bombs.

There are, then, tens of thousands of nuclear weapons in our world: weapons which can travel through the air (and into space), weapons which can be launched from the earth or from submarines. Within our own country, the fact that 41 states have some kind of nuclear weapon component, while 28 have nuclear weapons themselves, implies that no citizen of our country is more than a few hundred miles (at maximum) from nuclear weapons, no matter where she/he lives.

This reality has become poignantly clear to me within the past few months. In order to find the space and the grace in which to attempt to write a book about peacemaking and nuclear terror, I chose to spend several months in a somewhat remote but very beautiful section of the northern lower peninsula of Michigan. It is a very peaceful place, where God's creation speaks with special beneficence of the beauty of God and all that lives. The white-tailed deer are at home here. They visit my yard daily and sleep at night under a magnificent and graceful pine tree which my father planted many years ago. One lovely doe leads her fawns with particular care and motherly wisdom. Together we see sunsets, undimmed by smog, whose reflections in the clear, spring-fed lake invite one to extravagant imaginings of peace and of union.

Yet less than twenty miles from here is a major Air Force base which houses 150 nuclear bombs, 60 short-range attack missiles (SRAM), and 200 air-launched cruise missiles (ALCM).[20] There are many days when one sees a gentle, healing creation but hears the ominous sound of Air Force jets overhead. In even the most beautiful places on earth, there is no flight from the nuclear reality nor from the potential of nuclear destruction.

Nuclear Destruction

The potential for nuclear destruction, it must be noted, lies not only in a possible nuclear attack, but also in the ever-present possibility of nuclear accidents. Major nuclear accidents, involving "significant damage to the warhead or actual detonation of the high explosive trigger,"[21] are termed "broken arrows" by the Department of Defense. (Minor accidents are called "bent spears.") While reluctant to publish such incidents, in 1981, the Department of Defense did acknowledge 27 "broken arrows." One example suffices to show the dangers involved in such accidents. In this case, two nuclear bombs fell from a B-52 bomber which was itself coming apart. The parachute on one bomb opened; the other did not. The latter bomb broke apart but did not explode. A portion of that bomb which contained uranium was never recovered.[22]

What would happen if a nuclear warhead *did* explode? Although Hiroshima and Nagasaki provide sorrowful evidence of the destructive power of atomic weapons, this evidence is inadequate in terms of today's nuclear arsenals. Many people have become concerned about the aftermath of a nuclear explosion. Scientists, physicians, nurses, novelists, and even television writers have attempted to plot the effects. Increased consciousness of the disastrous effects of a nuclear conflict has served as a catalyst to awaken many people to the danger present in our world. One has only to consult the publications of the Union of Concerned Scientists, the Ground Zero organization,

the Physicians for Social Responsibility, or even those of the Department of Defense in order to find scholarly as well as graphic
predictions of what has been called — among other things —
"The Day After," or "Armageddon."[23]

The first effects of a nuclear attack of course would be immediate. They would also vary according to the size of the attack
and whether it was countervalue or counterforce. In any case,
the number of persons killed would be enormous. Few experts,
no matter what their position on nuclear weapons, speak of
"thousands" of dead; all speak of "millions." While the death of
millions and the massive destruction of property would be the
most obvious effects, other, more extended results would also be
felt. Illnesses resulting from exposure to massive doses of radiation; the destruction of means of survival such as food, medicine,
agriculture; genetic alterations; birth defects in following generations . . . all of these are predicted with certainty.

Further, any nuclear explosion would have global effects.
The mushroom cloud carries death within itself, and it moves
through the atmosphere carrying that death. The damage to the
ozone layer, to weather patterns — not to mention the chaos of
the global economy — would all be part of the aftermath. Ultimately, the results of a nuclear war could be total: the end of our
planet. The most poignant statement for me of the possible total
effect of nuclear war remains that of Jonathan Schell in his
work, *The Fate of the Earth*.

While flying between Detroit and Chicago one afternoon, I
looked out of the window of the plane and saw the earth below
me, bathed in sunshine, gleaming like a magic place. I then
opened a copy of *The New Yorker* (February 1, 1982), and read
the following:

> The annihilation of the belligerent nations would
> be a catastrophe beyond anything in history, but it
> would not be the end of the world. The destruction of
> human civilization, even without the biological de-

struction of the human species, may perhaps rightly be called the end of the world, since it would be the end of that sum of cultural achievements and human relationships which constitutes what many people mean when they speak of 'the world.' The biological destruction of mankind would, of course, be the end of the world in a stricter sense. As for the destruction of all life on the planet, it would be not merely a human but a planetary end — the death of the earth. And although the annihilation of other forms of life could hardly be of concern to human beings once they themselves had been annihilated, this more comprehensive, planetary termination is nevertheless full of sorrowful meaning for us as we reflect on the possibility now, while we still exist. We not only live on the earth but also are of the earth, and the thought of its death, or even of its mutilation, touches a deep chord in our nature.[24]

Arms Control

Premonitions of that "sorrowful meaning" have led people to work toward some kind of control over nuclear weapons since their first use — *before* their first use, in fact. Scientists involved in the Manhattan Project recognized the enormous destructive potential of atomic weapons. Under the leadership of James Franck and Leo Szilard, they submitted a report to the Secretary of the Navy on June 11, 1945, which urged that the bomb be exploded in a demonstration rather than in an actual attack against Japan. Such a demonstration, they felt, would show the Japanese (and the world) the enormous power which could be used against them and induce them to surrender.

Franck and his colleagues called for an international authority which would control atomic weapons; they also attemp-

ted to distinguish between political goals and military expe-
diency. The clear distinction of these two has plagued peoples
since that time. Several of the statements in this forty-year-old
document remain true today:

> In the past, science has often been able to provide
> new methods of protection against new weapons of
> aggression it made possible, but it cannot promise
> such efficient protection against the destructive use
> of nuclear power. This protection can come only from
> the political organization of the world. Among all the
> arguments calling for an efficient international or-
> ganization for peace, the existence of nuclear
> weapons is the most compelling one . . .

> We believe that these considerations make the use
> of nuclear bombs for an early unannounced attack
> against Japan inadvisable. If the United States were
> to be the first to release this new means of indiscrimi-
> nate destruction upon mankind, she would sacrifice
> public support throughout the world, precipitate the
> race for armaments, and prejudice the possibility of
> reaching an international agreement on the future
> control of such weapons.

> To sum up, we urge that the use of nuclear bombs
> in this war be considered as a problem of long-range
> national policy rather than of military expediency,
> and that this policy be directed primarily to the
> achievement of an agreement permitting an effective
> international control of the means of nuclear war.[25]

Obviously — and tragically — this view did not prevail.

The next attempt at arms control came with the presentation of the Baruch Plan to the United Nations in 1946. This plan
"called for the creation of an international nuclear authority and
a suitable system of safeguards after which the United States

would be obliged to dismantle its atomic bombs."[26] The Soviet Union, insisting that the United States dismantle its weapons before any agreement, rejected the proposal.

Since 1945, arms talks have been held sporadically, and several treaties have been signed.[27] Some of the most significant are: the Partial Test Ban Treaty (1963) which prohibits nuclear explosions in the atmosphere, the oceans, or space; the SALT I agreement (1972) which provides for a freeze in the deployment of some, but not all, new strategic nuclear weapons delivery systems; the SALT I ABM agreement (also 1972) which prohibits deployment of anti-ballistic missiles by the U. S. and the Soviet Union, with two exceptions on each side (one for defense of the nation's capital, and one for another ICBM site — this was later limited to a single site for each country). The SALT II treaty (1979), which has not been ratified by the U. S., was an attempt to set limits on numbers and categories of nuclear weapons.

The Outer Space Treaty (1967) prohibits all military activity in outer space, including the moon and other celestial bodies. The Strategic Defense Initiative, which will require the firing of an atomic bomb in order to activate the defense shield, poses problems for the honoring of this treaty. In addition, the SALT I ABM treaty would be broken by the introduction of a system designed to destroy ballistic missiles. In May, 1986, finally, the Administration announced its intention to no longer honor the SALT II treaty.

The most recent arms control talks, which began in Geneva in 1982 and which were intensified after the meeting between President Reagan and Premier Gorbachev in November, 1985, have not been marked by success, but rather by accusations and altercations. Premier Gorbachev's thrice-extended unilateral test ban has thrice been branded "propoganda" by the U. S. which continues underground nuclear testing. The number of weapons grows, the danger increases, and the cost of financing the arms race escalates.

Costs

In 1939, President Roosevelt directed that $6,000 be appropriated for research on atomic weapons.[28] The requests for military funding for the FY 1985 budget totalled $313.4 billion, including $60 billion for new weapons and $108 billion in weapons procurement.[29] On October 30, 1985, the House of Representatives passed a Defense Department spending bill totalling $292 billion. This amount is $10 billion less than the bill discussed in the Senate and $30 billion less than the administration had requested. It included $1.7 billion for the production of twelve new MX missiles and $2.5 billion for the Strategic Defense Initiative.[30]

As military expenditures have increased, the costs of nuclear weapons have been in more than the dollars paid for them. Money appropriated for defense spending must come from somewhere. Even a cursory glance at the national budgets for the past few years indicates two major sources: funds previously used for domestic programs such as education, medical assistance, child care, mass transit, etc.; and deficit spending. The actual budget outlay (i.e. the amount spent as opposed to the amount allocated) for the fiscal years 1982-1985 shows a $75.8 billion dollar decrease in major domestic programs, a $90 billion dollar increase in defense spending and, inevitably, a $30 billion dollar increase in interest payments on the national debt.[31]

The summer of 1985 witnessed a historic moment for the U.S. — the country became a debtor nation. The U. S. owes more than it takes in (and is able to pay back). A new 'ritual' has begun to take place in Congress: that of raising the debt ceiling. Periodically, it becomes evident that unless the government borrows more money, it has no way to pay its bills. The AP and the UPI report of November 15, 1985, reflects the commonplace character of this action:

WASHINGTON — The government's latest fiscal mess was cleaned up temporarily Thursday after the

House gave final congressional approval to interim legislation raising the national debt limit to $1.9 trillion [$1.9,000,000,000,000].

With no debate and only about two dozen members present, the House, on a voice vote, approved the legislation that postpones a credit crunch through Dec. 6 by raising the government's $1.824 trillion line of credit by $80 billion. It now goes to the White House, where President Reagan is expected to sign the measure.[32]

Nuclear arms are expensive. They are also very dangerous. The world seems unable to control their increase. These are facts, facts which emerge from even a brief review of the history of nuclear weapons. With Dorothee Soelle, we find ourselves benumbed and bewildered by the numbers, the sizes, the kilotons and megatons of nuclear weapons. With her, too, it becomes very difficult to understand the various strategies, targeting doctrines, distinctions, and costs. And yet we are told that peacemaking is a requirement of our faith!

The facts about nuclear arms, their "truth," it would seem, do not really make us free. Rather, they depress us, frighten us, separate us one from another. Overwhelmed, we want to ignore these facts, to make them go away. But we cannot. They are real. Freedom comes only when we face the truth, when we go beyond the numbers, the acronyms and the maps with targets marked in red.

The truth makes us free only when/if we take responsibility for it. Soelle understands this. She continues her reflection upon her own reactions to studying the arms race with these words:

> I do not want to see it and I do not want to hear it, and I'm not better than my fathers and my mothers in Germany who also told me when I asked them, "We didn't know." I don't want this to happen again. I

don't want my children coming to me and saying,
"Now, what did you do," and me saying, "I didn't
know."[33]

Perhaps the first step in taking responsibility is to ask what
the facts *mean*. What does the presence of so many weapons in
so many places mean to us and to all peoples? Scientists have
calculated what a nuclear explosion would do to the earth. (The
tragic incident at Chernobyl in the summer of 1986 has given us
a dire warning.) But what does the simple presence of these
weapons do to us now? How much, really, have nuclear weapons
cost us, and how much have they already hurt every human
being alive on this our earth, our home? Chapter Two will seek
some answers to these questions.

2
"Please Tell Me"
THE COST OF
NUCLEAR WEAPONS

In 1983, the Pax Christi groups in the Detroit area collaborated with the theology departments of the Roman Catholic colleges to sponsor a competition among the students of Catholic junior-high and high schools. The students were invited to write to the world's leaders asking them to work for peace. These letters were ultimately collected in a small booklet. The first letter in that booklet is poignantly illustrative of the world's malaise. A young woman wrote: "Dear Sirs, I am in the eleventh grade and am beginning to make serious plans for my future. Please tell me if I am wasting my time."[1]

This young woman's sad question leads us to the meaning behind the facts of nuclear weapons. Such weapons cost billions of dollars, we all know that; but they cost even more in terms of the social fabric of our country and, most tragically, in terms of the hearts and minds of our people. How can it be that a young girl, filled with promise, is forced to wonder if she wastes her time planning for a future? What has the presence and production of nuclear weapons done to her and to millions like her? What do the billions of dollars and intense concentration on weapons production do to other aspects of our society? What happens to us who live in the company of these weapons, who hear the jets overhead and wonder what they carry? Chapter

Two seeks to examine the costs of the arms race both to society
at large and to the individual human person.

Social Costs

During the process of writing the Pastoral, the Bishops'
committee met with Secretary of Defense Caspar Weinberger at
his office in the Pentagon. In the course of the meeting, the question of the effects of the arms buildup on the economy was discussed. The Secretary spoke of the numbers of jobs being
created in the defense industry. He said that people working in
defense were not on welfare roles, and described this fact as a
"serendipitous fallout." His words were not only macabre (how
can a "fallout" ever be "serendipitous"?), they were also very
misleading.

It is often said that the defense industry creates jobs and
thus helps the economy. This is simply not the case, however,
for several reasons. In the first place, the type of work created
requires highly skilled and well-educated employees. The problem of unemployment is most strongly felt among the unskilled
or semi-skilled laborers. It is difficult to envision an increase in
technical jobs helping the minority worker, the inner city black
youth, the single mother. The defense industry does not help
those most in need of employment.

In the second place, more jobs would be created if the money
spent in the defense industry were to be applied to other areas.
If the amount of money spent on a single B-1 bomber (at its 1977
price) were used in the housing industry, for example, 30,000
jobs would be created; if applied to welfare and public works,
20,000 jobs would result. Bruce Russett, in *The Prisoners of Insecurity: Nuclear Deterrence, The Arms Race, and Arms Control*,[2] refers to the number of jobs which would either be created
or lost by a 30 percent change in the defense budget. If the
budget were raised 30 percent, and there was a concomitant
drop of 30 percent in health, public assistance, and environmen-

tal programs, 1,300,000 jobs would be lost. If, however, defense lost 30 percent and the others were raised, 2,000,000 jobs would be created. Seven hundred thousand more jobs would be created because of the difference in types of jobs and in salaries. Russett cites four studies, each done differently from the others, which point to the same conclusion. "Military spending produces fewer jobs than does virtually any other kind of spending, private or public (except for the space programs)."[3]

Further, the dollars spent in weapons production are dead-end dollars. They do not return to the economy. Weapons, particularly nuclear weapons, are made for the purpose of *non*-use. All other products are meant to be used, worn out, and replaced with new ones. A car, a winter coat, an appliance must all be eventually replaced after extended use. If nuclear weapons are ever used, there will be no replacements.

In addition, there are hidden costs to society in the arms race, one of which is the loss of highly-skilled, creative persons to other enterprises. Between 30 and 50 percent of all the scientists and engineers in this country work in the military sector, creating and refining instruments of destruction.[4] What if these same talents and energies were expended on creating and refining the nation's systems of transportation or education. What if they were applied to medicine. The enterprise of higher education is harmed by the defense industry, not helped by it. The higher salaries attainable in defense have lured away from the universities a generation of professors skilled in areas such as computer technology. We are rapidly approaching a time when there will be no one to teach a new generation.[5]

Increased defense spending does not help the economy in the areas where help is most necessary. It diverts talent from other, important sectors of our society, and it produces an atmosphere of greed and corruption within the industry itself. We have recently become conscious that the defense industry has taken on aspects of a law unto itself. Vast amounts of money are spent with little supervision or concern. Sloppy accounting, sometimes blatant dishonesty, appear to be the norm among defense contractors. We all know of the stories of the astronomically priced wrenches, coffee pots, and ashtrays. We have all read of the tax dollars spent for entertainment and "jaunts" for important persons.

There is a new expression in our vocabulary these days: "cost overrun." Weapons and equipment frequently cost the nation several times their original estimates. For example, the cost overrun (to 1981) of the U.S. Navy's current submarine, frigate, and destroyer programs was $42 billion dollars. This same amount, if used by the state of California, could have provided "a ten year investment to spur solar energy for space-, water-, and industrial-process heating; this would involve 376,000 new jobs and lead to vast fuel savings."[6] Other examples abound. Three will suffice: up to 1981, the overrun on the Navy's Trident submarine and the Air Force's F-16 programs was $33 billion; the Navy's F-18 aircraft program reached $26.4 billion; the Army's UH-60A helicopter program was $4.7 billion.[7]

Billions of dollars and a fervor for and fascination with new weapons create a climate where neither buyer nor seller is concerned about price and where integrity is all too often a rare commodity. Recent months have witnessed a series of indictments and charges of corruption which have reached into the highest levels of our country's government. The indictment in December, 1985, of the director of NASA is but one sorry example. And all of the money involved in this comes from U. S. tax dollars. General Dynamics will not go bankrupt from these expenses. *We* will.

The example of cost overruns, seen in relation to other uses to which that money could be put, leads us to even more hidden costs — and more painful ones. How does such spending affect the needy among us, those not exposed to "serendipitous fallout?"

We have seen that domestic spending has decreased in recent years by at least $75 billion. The combination of a decrease in domestic funding and a rapid increase in military expenditures is a unique phenomenon. Russett points out that in the years from 1940-1979, the general pattern of government expenditures was one in which health and education spending increased at the same time as did military spending. "This happened in 21 of the 39 years, and in only two years did health and education spending go down when military spending rose. . . . The patterns tended to be the same under Republican presidents as under Democratic ones."[8]

Since 1979, however, health and education spending have consistently gone down while military spending has continued to rise. This phenomenon has significant ramifications in terms of the national priorities. It indicates that weapons and defense take priority over the health and education of our citizens, especially those most in need of assistance. Cuts in Medicaid, for example, directly affect the lives of millions of persons. One must ask — no matter what the answer — whether $25 billion in the 1986 budget was better spent for the year's MX missile program, or to rescind the proposal to freeze the cost of living adjustments in Social Security and other pension payments. This proposal, according to Seymour Melman in the New York *Times,* "would push 420,000 people [elderly people!] into poverty."[9]

Melman offers other examples of choices in the use of parallel amounts of funding: to build 800 Army multiple launch rockets at the cost of $8.7 million *or* reinstate the proposed 1986-87 cuts in federal funding for subsidized lunches for New York city school children; the price of one projected Marine amphibious assault ship ($1.5 billion) *or* proposed federal cuts in housing for elderly and handicapped and cuts in energy assistance for poor people ($1.5 billion); to spend $5.3 billion for the Army's single-channel ground and air-borne radio system *or* to spend the same amount for a one-third increase in funding for the federal school lunch program, food stamp program, and Women, Infants and Children program.[10]

It is, admittedly, somewhat simplistic to place what are complex choices dealing with the hundreds of elements of a national budget in such bald parallels. These parallels do exist, however, and taken together they do say something. They say that a trend has begun, which leads to a choice of weapons over people — over the quality of the lives of millions of women, men, and children. And all of this is done in the name of and for the avowed purpose of defending and protecting these same people.

Dwight Eisenhower warned of this decades ago: "Every gun that is made, every warship launched, every rocket fired signifies, in the final sense, a theft from those who hunger and are not fed, those who are cold and not clothed. This world in arms is not spending money alone. It is spending the sweat of its laborers, the genius of its scientists, the hopes of its children."[11] President Carter recognized this in 1977, when he declared that "the nations of the world spent [in 1976] more than sixty times as much equipping each soldier as we did in educating each child."[12]

On a recent visit to Ireland, I became acquainted with the tragedy of the Irish famine of 1845-48. I had heard many stories about the famine; my own ancestors had come to North America in its wake. In Ireland, itself, however, especially among the deserted, nearly destroyed "famine houses" of West Cork, I began to sense the enormity of the loss of that time.

Potatoes (along with an occasional pig) were all that most people had to eat. They were fairly nutritious and could be grown in small areas. Many people survived the first year of the famine; but, when blight ruined the potato crop for a second time, the starving people ate the seed potatoes intended for the next year's planting. When they did this they destroyed their future, for there was nothing left with which to begin anew.

When the world spends sixty times as much to equip a soldier as it does to educate a child, when scientists and scholars are encouraged to use their talents in military industries rather than in the education and the challenge of new generations, one can only wonder at the famine which awaits us.

Personal Costs

Not everyone in Ireland starved, obviously, and not everyone in the U. S. consciously suffers from the arms race. Anyone who pays taxes, of course, pays for military spending; but for many this is not a *conscious* burden. In fact, for those who believe in nuclear weapons and in a "strong defense," such payment is well worth the cost.

There are, however, still greater costs, ones hidden even more deeply than numbers in federal budgets. These are the costs each of us carries in our own hearts and minds. Every person alive since August 6, 1945, shares this world with nuclear weapons. What does *this* fact do to us? The following statement is undeniably true: "Each of you awakens each day to a world that could be annihilated at any moment."[13] What does *this* cost us?

None of us wants to think about a nuclear war, yet each of us does. The possibility lurks surprisingly close to the surface in our minds and makes itself felt at moments with an intensity which stuns us. A few years ago, while talking with three leaders of religious women, I heard of an experience they shared while in Rome. These women were meeting with Vatican officials the day of the Papal assassination attempt. During this meeting, they heard guns being fired, screams, sirens and helicopters flying overhead. The first thought of each of these women was that a nuclear war had begun. This was their instinctive reaction, the surfacing of their ever-present, never very dormant fear.

Shortly after this conversation, I knew a somewhat similar experience. One of the former U.S. Secretaries of Defense who agreed to speak to the Bishops' committee met with us at the United States Catholic Conference offices on Massachusetts Avenue in Washington, D.C. He spoke eloquently about the vulnerability of the U.S. Command, Control, Communications, Information network (C_3I) and elaborated upon the certainty that one of the first targets for the enemy would be the headquarters of this country's political and military leaders. The Secretary explained the existing C_3I structures, and told us how inadequate they were.

The sense of the vulnerability of Washington, D.C., slowly became very real to me, and I began to experience a feeling of genuine terror. I sat in that quiet room in the heart of the city and struggled with a terrible desire to run from that place, to flee that city, to pray to the "God of the Gaps" to save me from this horrifying danger. I did not run, obviously, but I was never again carefree as I approached the nation's capital.

Each of us can tell of her/his own moments of nuclear terror. Perhaps they came while watching a film or reading an article, perhaps in the question of a child or in a dream. These moments pass, but psychologists tell us that the terror does not, for the threat is real.

Robert J. Lifton has made a long and serious study of the psychological effects of living with nuclear weapons. He began by working with survivors of Hiroshima and Nagasaki. Lifton recognized many recurring themes among the testimony of the survivors which led him to conclude that humankind has gone through "a historical shift from Victorian struggles concerning sexuality and moralism to our present preoccupation with absurd death (and by implication, absurd life) and unlimited technological violence."[14] Central to this shift is the change in the imagery for life and death; more specifically, one's capacity to symbolize immortality and thus express one's historical and biological continuity. Hiroshima and Nagasaki precipitated this shift because these events radically altered our death imagery from that of individual death (with its possibilities for some type of immortality/continuity) to that of total annihilation (with its implication of futurelessness). The spectre of annihilation has profoundly influenced the life of every woman, man and child who has been alive in our world since August 6, 1945.

Michael Carey, one of Lifton's assistants, studied the effects of nuclear weapons on a group of forty men and women who were in their twenties and thirties in the mid-1970s.[15] He found a sequence of attitudes in terms of relating to the bomb, as well as a recurring set of themes. Many of us will recognize our own experience in Carey's descriptions.

The first stage, experienced by the young child at the time of entering school, is one of "amorphous death anxiety."[16] The participants in the study remembered the drills which were meant to teach them how to respond to the bomb: pull down the window shades, get under the desk, go to the basement in an orderly fashion, file into the corridor and face the interior walls. Such drills made the children aware of "the bomb", a mysterious yet deadly thing which could destroy the whole world. This awareness entered into their dreams as images of violence and destruction which were made more terrifying by the dreamers' inability to reach family members or air raid shelters.

The second stage was marked by "sustained numbing."[17] In early adolescence, the whole issue seemed to fade away and the participants appeared to forget about the bomb. The frightening dreams continued, however, and the imagery of extinction was often very close to the surface.

Late adolescence and early adulthood gave witness to a wide continuum of responses ranging from obsession with the bomb, to concern about it, to claims that it had little or no influence. Yet further probing revealed the continuing presence of images related to annihilation.

These would often include the sense that one's own life or the lives of one's children would end violently and prematurely, or a back-and-forth, contradictory pattern between numbness toward the whole ques-

tion and periodic experience of anxiety (which could
be stimulated by external nuclear threats or old personal fears); or else the more vague sense of living
under a nuclear shadow that did not seem to deter-
mine any specific life decision but would never quite
go away either.[18]

These stages are elaborately described and taken to their
most radical conclusion in Tim O'Brien's 1985 novel, *The Nuclear Age*.[19] As a young boy, William, the "hero" of the novel,
takes *very* seriously what he learns about the bomb. He attempts to build a shelter in his basement and is forced to recognize that it is useless against an attack. He knows the nightmares and the visions of the end that Carey describes, and
gradually becomes involved in the activist movements of the sixties. At the time of the composition of the novel, William is prosperous, married, father of a daughter. But his nuclear nightmares haunt him still. He decides to build a shelter in his back-
yard. Beginning with a shovel, he eventually turns to dynamite
to make the hole big enough. In the process, William finds it
necessary to imprison both his wife and daughter. They are convinced he has gone mad. What began as a plan to protect them
evolves into their death sentence. William decides to blow all of
them up — in the bomb shelter — so that they will not have to
face the nuclear holocaust. The madness of our time is reflected
in the madness of a man who would kill that which he most loves
in order to save it from death.

The themes which emerged from this study will also "not go
away." The first of these is that of the equation of death with annihilation. The great human struggle to face the reality of one's
own death becomes terribly exacerbated by the possibility that
one's death will be part of the total extinction of everything. This
painful phenomenon becomes even more grievous when we remember that little children must face their own death/annihila-
tion, even before they have begun to learn about living.

A sense of the unmanageability of life accompanies the first theme; one feels "that any attempt to order existence is countered by the possibility of its absolute interruption."[20] A further theme is that of "the perception of craziness." Both the making of nuclear weapons and the proposed methods of protection against them are perceived as absurd. One is introduced to "the sense of the world as mad," says Lifton.[21] This recognition of "radical absurdity" can lead some to identify with the bomb itself. One's own craziness is joined to that of the bomb, leading to a wish that it would be dropped so that one might see the spectacle and put an end to all of the wondering.

There is a final theme: the double life. One side of the person lives an ordinary life, going through the normal stages of growth and development. There is always, however, the "other half," the imagery of annihilation. The costs become enormous, psychic numbing invades our lives. "Psychic numbing," a term coined by Lifton during his work with atomic bomb survivors, leads one to deaden or numb feelings in order to be able to get on with "normal" life. Everyone experiences this at times, especially when emergencies arise or one is faced with overwhelmingly painful information.

Psychic numbing can be a healthy form of self-preservation. It can enable us to carry on, to endure the first awful moments of what could be a devastating situation. If it continues for too long a time or becomes permanent, however, psychic numbing is very destructive for several reasons. One begins to lead a double life, as Lifton says, and the inherent contradictions in such a manner of existing inevitably take their toll. Further, to numb one's feelings means to numb them *all*. Pain may be mitigated, but so are joy and wonder, compassion and love. Finally, a gap occurs — and grows — between knowledge and feeling. Such a separation can lead to disastrous consequences not only for the individual, but also for anyone affected by that individual's decisions. Life and death issues can not be adequately decided when knowledge is devoid of sensitivity and feeling.

The shape of human existence has altered drastically since August 6, 1945, and the insidious, pervasive nuclear threat affects all stages of that existence — from childhood to death. It is especially the radical shift in our image of death that has so profoundly and grievously changed our lives. Every human person seeks for some type of immortality, some way in which our spirit continues after we are no longer physically present. For most people, continuity is attained through children. Succeeding generations will carry on the name, the spirit, something of ourselves. Others strive to create that which will endure: the 'Great American Novel,' a poem, magnificent music, a system of law, a scientific discovery. Still others seek to build something: a cathedral, the world's tallest skyscraper, a beautiful memorial, a school. Some choose to give their lives in service of human kind so that the world will be a better place and one will live on in the hearts of those who reap the benefits of our sacrifice.

In the face of annihilation, none of these actions has any meaning. Death as extinction implies the death of all that one hopes to leave behind as a sign that one has lived in this world and somehow made a difference. There are few scenarios more sorrowful than that of dying alone and unmourned. Perhaps the most grief-provoking aftermath of the tragic plane crash off the coast of Ireland in July, 1985, was the burial in Cork City of seven bodies which had never been claimed. How, we ask ourselves, can anyone die and have no one to miss them? Annihilation means nothing left, no one to mourn. Hopefully, it will never take place; but its imagery has already invaded our individual and collective psyches, frightening us, wounding us, diminishing us. And our world shows it. "Please tell me if I am wasting my time."

The most natural reaction to such terror is to seek to escape it. Many attempt to do so through drugs or forgetful hedonism; others seek transcendental experiences of one type or another. If one can find another place or space, then perhaps one can endure. Some individuals take this search quite literally. In *Star*

Warriors,[22] William J. Broad quotes a brilliant young scientist deeply involved in the Star Wars/SDI research. "What I want more than anything is essentially to get the human race into space. It's the future. If you stay down here, some disaster is going to strike and you're going to be wiped. If you get into space and spread out, there's just no chance of the human race disappearing."[23] With his statement, the young scientist reflects the influence of one of our nation's fundamental myths. Since the founding of this country, we have been engaged in the conquering of new frontiers: the West, technological frontiers, societal ones, and finally, that of space. The group which most vocally supports Star Wars calls itself "The High Frontier." His statement also reflects both the despair and the absurdity of our times. The only hope for the future of humankind is to escape from the world. One who works on weapons which will be used in space advocates not merely living in space, but moving the human race into space.

Not everyone plans to move into space, however; most of us try to resolve the dilemma here on earth. Faced with terrifying insecurity, we search for alternatives which will make us secure. Two closely connected ones are particularly appealing; fundamentalism and nuclearism. In response to the sense that everything is threatened, there is a tendency to search for, name, and embrace the fundamentals, the essential beliefs and doctrines which provide a sense of continuity, order, and security. This search for fundamentals becomes fundamental*ism* when, in the restatement of the fundamentals, the words themselves become literal and immutable; they are held to be sacred and unchangeble.[24] These words, then, cannot be questioned or interpreted, for all interpretation implies multidimensional meaning. Literal translation is concerned not with conveying meaning as with replacing one set of words with another literal set of words. The "fundamentals" never change, never develop, and thus never provide challenge to growth. The security they provide is a static one, and one which inevitably becomes anachronistic. Fundamentalism lead inevitably to rigidity and to diminishment, for it renounces mystery even as it repudiates questions.

It is not surprising, then, that nuclear terror provokes a resurgence in all types of fundamentalism. Political fundamentalism runs rampant in our land. Terms such as "freedom, liberty, democracy," are taken as sacred and they all carry only one meaning. They are unambiguous and unquestionable. Those who question either definition or manifestation are viewed as misguided and naive, or conspirators and perhaps communists. Closely allied to political fundamentalism is another, more virulent strain of the same malaise: nuclearism.

Lifton and Richard Falk insist that nuclearism is a disease. They define it as "psychological, political, and military dependence on nuclear weapons, the embrace of the weapons as a solution to a wide variety of human dilemmas, most ironically that of 'security.' "[25] Nuclear weapons have become the new, sacred, fundamentals. They alone will save us, either because their very existence will prevent war, or because they will enable us to overcome in war. Nuclearism relies on weapons to save the world, rather than treaties or diplomacy or negotiation. Nothing must stop the technological advancements in weapons design — not cost, not danger, not even questions of feasibility or practicality. William Broad quotes another Star Warrior, one who does not want to be known as a "bomb maker" but as a "weapons designer," and who calls nuclear weapons "weapons of life." In a discussion of the super-computers being developed at the Livermore laboratory, the scientist said, "I consider computers to be as much a weapon as nuclear warheads are . . . They have as much importance to the *salvation of society*. They can save millions of lives." (italics mine)[26]

If nuclear weapons are perceived as sacred and as the source of our national security, then anyone who questions or challenges their value, let alone their existence, is not merely expressing a different opinion. She/he is threatening the security and is, at some deep level, a blasphemer. The extent to which nuclearism and political fundamentalism have invaded our country shows itself in the growing tendency to treat peace activists as a greater threat than perpetrators of both white collar and violent crimes.

There is a long train which travels throughout our country. It is called the "White Train," even though it has recently been painted black in order to be less easy to identify. This train travels in secrecy; its routes are never announced. It is heavily armed and it carries nuclear weapons. Since people have begun to track and to publicize the route of the train, the Department of Energy has proposed regulations which would ban any publicizing of "Unclassified Controlled Nuclear Information" (UCNI), including information about the transportation of nuclear weapons. "These proposed regulations bear a civil penalty of a $100,000 fine imposed by the Secretary of Energy and a criminal penalty of 20 years in prison."[27]

Multiple accounts in the media informed us that on May 21, 1985, the Secretary of the Navy charged that General Dynamics Corporation was guilty of misconduct and incorrect billing practices to the amount of $75 million. The company was suspended and $22.5 million in contracts were cancelled. But no fines were levied; no one went to prison. In fact, the Pentagon awarded $700 million in new contracts to the same company on August 13, 1985. Those who make nuclear weapons and who cheat the government (and the people) out of millions of dollars are treated with greater compassion than those who act in opposition to those weapons.

Even violent crime is sometimes viewed as less dangerous than peace activity. In December, 1983, two legal processes which affected my religious community took place within approximately twenty miles of each other. One was the preliminary hearing in a first-degree murder case; the other was the trial of nine persons who had trespassed by entering onto the parking lot of a munitions company and kneeling down to pray. In the former process, one of our Sisters had been the victim; in

the latter, three of our Sisters were among those on trial. At the
hearing for the murder trial there were two to three armed deputies in the room. The defendant, accused of robbing, shooting
(at very close range), and killing a gifted and caring 49-year-old
woman, entered the courtroom carefully groomed, neatly
dressed, and carrying books and papers, unhampered by hand-
cuffs. At the trial of the other nine persons, approximately fifteen armed deputies were present in the room and the defen-
dants entered the court in jail uniforms and in chains. To witness both scenes was to find oneself deeply and painfully at the
heart of the absurdity of our time. Is peacemaking really more
threatening than murder? Perhaps this is a clue as to why
peacemaking is a requirement of our *faith*.

Nuclearism, with its irrational promise of security based
upon the very weapons which have made all of creation insecure
and vulnerable, is often closely allied with the most visible form
of fundamentalism of our time: the religious. The resurgence of
religious fundamentalism is not surprising. For most people,
the security of a set of beliefs is the ultimate security, the one
which remains when all else fails. Today we witness a "moral
majority" movement which calls all Americans to renewed faith
in God, in the American way, and in nuclear weapons. We hear
speeches and read articles and books which rail against "godless
communism" in all its nefarious manifestations including gay
rights activities, anti-apartheid movements, liberation struggles, and the peace movement. It is not only right that we should
stand ready to defend our country at any cost and for any reason,
it is moral and even holy. One's intelligence is not only involved,
one's character and moral correctness become part of the debate
and the judgment.

Religion traditionally provides people with unshakable images of immortality in terms of some form of life after death. If
we do not live on in our children or our works, then at least we
will know the immortality of a heaven or hell. But here too the
nuclear terror makes itself felt and questions are posed which

go to the very core of our faith. With a unique intensity, people again ask the ultimate questions: Who is God? Where is God? And the answers are not easily found in a world and a time threatened with annihilation. "The more general principle may well be that as death imagery comes to take the shape of total annihilation or extinction, religious symbolism becomes both more sought after and more inadequate."[28] We need God/security more than ever, it seems, and yet the usual ways of finding that God and of resting secure in our faith are themselves threatened to the core by nuclear terror.

A very common image of the world's end is that of the final judgment. This judgment has two main scenarios: God returns to earth and judges between the good and evil, saving the good while condemning the evil; or, a final, fatal battle rages in which the evil perish, the good conquer. This *image* of a final battle, frequently called Armageddon after the biblical story of a heavenly war (Rev. 16:16), is often translated into the *reality* of a nuclear war. Nuclear war is then seen as God's judgment whereby "they" (evil ones, communists, perverts, etc.) will be destroyed and "we" (good ones, Americans, capitalists, perhaps even some allies) will be saved.

There are two (at least!) serious problems with this way of imaging immortality, however. In the first place, any realistic understanding of the effects of nuclear war show that there will no longer be a "we" or "they." Nuclear warheads do not distinguish the moral righteousness of their targets — they simply destroy. Secondly, it is not God who has made nuclear weapons, nor will it be God who uses them. Human beings have created these instruments of death; human beings have used them twice. If the world is destroyed by these weapons, it will be human beings who destroy it (and themselves) — not God.

Armageddon doesn't work. Nor do our accepted images of God. Many, many times when I have spoken with groups about war and peacemaking, someone asks: "Do you really think God will let this happen?" That question comes from genuine anguish. How could God let this happen? What kind of God would let the earth be destroyed? If I cannot trust *God* to save us, whom can I trust? Is God an uncaring, abstract principle which is not concerned about us? No, we say, of course not!

Yet, at the same time, if we are honest, we are compelled to remember two things: God has given us free will and we can and have used that will for evil as well as good; God is not a magician who makes things like nuclear weapons disappear. So we must ask, who is God and where, in the name of God, is God? And, in asking this we also ask, who, in the name of God, am I?

And all the while we continue to lead double lives: eating, sleeping, laughing, weeping, loving, preparing for the future, fearing every once in a while that the world has gone mad and we with it.

Nuclear weapons cost. They cost us money, they cost us creativity and hope. They drain our resources and diminish the already undervalued among us. They make us numb and give us nightmares. They force us to question our most cherished beliefs, our deepest, most sacred images. They tempt us and they terrify. The truth is no longer merely difficult to grasp, it is literally unbearable, and all the more so because it is no longer outside ourselves, but in us and of us. And peacemaking is a requirement of our faith.

There is call to grace in this impasse. Above all, there is call to conversion — conversion, not escape. All calls to conversion carry mirrors with them which show us ourselves as we are, even as they hint at who we could be. Transforming grace invites us to look at both. Who are we that we have come to this situation? Who could we become? Chapter Three begins to approach the mirror.

3
"Believing Our Own Logic"
PATTERNS THAT MAKE
FOR WAR

One of the experts who testified before the Bishops' committee was a retired high-ranking military officer. He spoke at length about the unrestrained growth of nuclear weapons and about their military uselessness. He also issued a dire warning when he stated: "We are beginning to believe our own logic." Even a casual acquaintance with the "logic" of nuclear weapons and the arms race gives clear evidence of the "world gone mad" of which Robert J. Lifton speaks so often. Believing our own logic, however, is but one of the dangerous patterns which encourages the cultivation of violence, the making of wars, the cost of nuclear weapons.

Once we acknowledge these dreadful costs, we are inevitably led to ask two basic questions: How did we reach this impossible situation? How do we get beyond it? It is with these questions, I believe, that the first stirrings of conversion are felt and life begins to assert itself in the midst of the threat of annihilation. In the very questioning we are challenged and led from the secure (if often deadly) realm of "knowing the facts" into the frightening yet exhilirating way of searching. I am convinced, further, that the search must begin in our collective mirror. Who are *we,* citizens of the United States at the end of the twentieth century, that we have reached such an impasse?

The answer to that question is not an easy one, nor can it ever be complete. Each person alive contributes to the "we," and each choice we make enhances or detracts from our identity. That identity, further, is profoundly affected by our individual and collective history. Who we are in this country at this time, and how we view the world, depends a great deal upon who we *were* and from whence we have come. We live with innumerable, rarely examined, inherited assumptions. They surround us, they identify us, they may also destroy us.

Perhaps the most basic assumption is that of our identity as a nation. Young in the world's history, this country began in the search for freedom and was unhampered by many of the inherited restrictions (such as strict, long-standing class distinctions) of older, more rigidly structured societies. Our ancestors came to a vast and beautiful land, struggled with great privations and created a new life and a new society. From the beginning, these persons were conscious of the special qualities of society in the "New World" and of the special gifts of life here. Viewing themselves as a new chosen people, the founders of this country saw the country as a new promised land. The fundamental myth of the United States came into being very quickly, and has remained foundational to our national consciousness ever since. Robert Benne and Philip Hefner articulate this myth in a three-fold manner: "To shake free of the limiting past, in a struggling ascent, toward the realization of promise in an open, gracious future. . . ."[1]

Coming to this country from a "limiting past" of religious intolerance or poverty or discrimination, men and women have struggled to make life better for themselves and for their children. Each generation was to be more prosperous, more cultivated than the last, each person was to have a more fulfilled life. And the greatness of the country, with its vast expanse of land and its seemingly unlimited wealth, made the dream very possible. The future was truly unlimited. The myth served to identify us even as it molded our vision for our own future. For many people the myth was true, and their lives reflected it. Ours is seen as a good country where freedom and justice are honored, where the rights of the individual are cherished. We are perceived (and we perceive ourselves) as a people who govern ourselves with integrity, who respect the rights of others, and who will defend freedom wherever it stands in jeopardy. Two World Wars have shown our willingness to sacrifice for our values, even as they have demonstrated our strength and our power. Although Vietnam surfaced widespread doubts about our power and our methods of defending freedom, most Americans continue to assume that this country is the "greatest nation on earth."

Most of this is true, but it is not all of the truth. There are other aspects to our identity, what Benne and Hefner call "the dark side of the myth."[2] Not everyone came to this country to shake off a limiting past, not everyone found freedom, many found slavery, many more experienced massive discrimination. Those who already lived here met with destruction and brutal, murderous oppression. Not everyone in our country has made the struggling ascent, and the future is neither so open nor so gracious as we would like to believe.

At the heart of our national myth, at the core of its dark side lies a basic, age-old, seemingly unshakable assumption which cries out for serious examination. Our identity, our "we," the values we cherish, the behavior we honor, has always been defined by a minority of "us." Certain values, models, modes of behavior have emerged and have shaped our national ethos. These have been formulated by those in charge, by the experts, the teachers, priests, philosophers, and national leaders: in other words, by white men. The public, dominant value system of the United States has been and continues to be masculine. It is the masculine model which forms our national consciousness, which dictates our modes of behavior and our ways of thinking. The impasse we have reached and the terror we share are indications that such a one-sided world-view is inadequate and, in fact, extremely dangerous.

The books proliferate, the studies abound. The nation is bankrupt, we are told, and not only in terms of the national debt. In our hearts, which tread carefully at the edge of terror and of despair, we suspect that there may be truth in these statements, even though we long to continue to view ourselves as "#1." Many among us, especially those who have formulated, defined, and now feel bound to protect the dominant value/behavior system, would choose to ignore the crisis among us or to blame the crisis rather than its causes. Ignorance is no longer possible, however, and blame always remains ineffective. Every aspect of our individual and collective lives has been shaped and warped by the one-sided world view in which most of us were raised. This world view, I contend, has produced the terror in which we live and is inadequate for its healing. The white male value system and the behavior patterns it promotes, if left unchecked and unexamined, enable and encourage the growth of terror and the danger of annihilation. There are four areas of our lives which are fundamental to our functioning and pivotal to the making of peace, yet each of these areas, when dominated by the male ethos, serves against peace. These four areas are: language, logic, power, and relationship.

Language

A few years ago, while teaching a course on Jesus' parables, I came across a line by Amos Wilder which startled me at the time and which now haunts me. "The language of a people is its fate," Wilder wrote, speaking of the language of early Christianity.[3] Even a cursory examination of nuclear language portends a sad fate for the people who use it.

Language is our means of communication, our most general way of knowing and being known. Through and in it we discover ourselves, each other, and our universe. As human beings we feel ourselves called to name reality (Gen 2:19-20). This is not a task to be taken lightly. To name is to identify and call forth the reality in that which stands before us as mystery; to name is to enter into relationship with that which is named. Little wonder people have always feared to name the divine even as they have longed to do so!

Language is more than a vehicle for naming, however; it also shapes the namer. For it is by means of language that a people learns its values and its desired modes of behavior. Children absorb the language of their elders and thus the values of the culture into which they are born. For example, when an American child misbehaves, she is likely to be told to "be good;" whereas when a French child does so, she is likely to be admonished to "sois sage" (be *wise*). Such admonitions, which are so quickly absorbed, direct us in our behavior, form our image of meaningful adulthood, and are extremely difficult to change when a new consciousness arises.

Language is not merely a chief means of communication, nor a fundamental instrument in the formation of the young; it is the identity of a people. One need only study a foreign language to realize this. Each language has its own character,mystery and personality. Governments can rise or fall on the issue of language. Oppressors know this and frequently forbid the use of native languages — Gaelic in Ireland, Catalan in Spain, tribal languages in African countries. If they do not forbid them, they demean them by making the oppressor's language the "official" one which everyone must speak if they are to function in the society. The oppressed recognize this action immediately and often keep their language alive at the cost of their lives. They do so because their language is who they are; it is their heritage.

The profound connection between language, identity, and oppression became very real to me when I was a student in Belgium. Belgium is a dual-language country (Flemish and French), and French had long been the dominant language. It was the language of law, finance, and higher education. The University students began to protest conditions at the Universities, including and especially the discrimination against the Flemish language. The government collapsed, laws were passed, and changes were made. I began my studies at the Universite Catholique de Louvain, and finished them at the Katholieke Universiteit te Leuven. The city in which I lived went from the primarily French-speaking Louvain to the Flemish Leuven, and the shop keepers, train conductors, mail carriers, waitresses, post office employees all refused to speak French. The Flemish language which had previously declared its speakers to be second-class citizens was now proudly, openly, *finally* the official language of the city. The city was their city now, a *Flemish* city.

The language of a people is its identity; it carries and continues the heritage even as it points to the future and fate of that same people. We are revealed by our language, and the ways in which we transform it in light of new experience and changed consciousness are perhaps most revelatory of all. Changes in a people's language indicate that something new has happened among them, that something new awaits them. Nuclear weapons have transformed the world's language. This transformation reveals much about who we are and what is our fate.

When the Bishops' committee began to meet with defense experts, government officials, and weapons specialists, it became clear to me that I was in the process of learning a whole new language, with its own grammar and syntax. Many of the terms were new to me (counterforce, countervalue, launch-on warning); the acronyms were sometimes baffling (MAD, MIRV, MARV, FEBA, PK, C_3I); the sentences seemed bizarre ("Modern war becomes disproportionate before it becomes indiscriminate"). I struggled to learn the terms, decipher the acronyms, follow the sentences which these men used. As I did so, a profound uneasiness gripped me, a sense of absurdity: I was in wonderland and language was standing on its head. Confrontation with nuclear language was for me a first step in the realization that peacemaking involved much more than protesting against a weapons system or a governmental policy. Nuclear language told me that war and peace are deeply ingrained in the fabric of our lives. The proclivity for either resides in the deepest part of our identity, and our identity as "Americans" is bound to war, not peace. Only an honest look into the mirror of our souls can change this. If it is not changed, we may not have another chance.

Nuclear weapons and the language which speaks of them have not merely introduced new terms such as "nuke" and "overkill," they have begun to pervert the language itself. The complex system of symbols that is the American/English language is being radically altered. Positive images become menacing: mushrooms which are good things to eat and the fabled home of magical elves; clouds, source of beauty and imagination for children, poets, and painters are combined to become "the mushroom cloud" — symbol of annihilation. Deadly images are made whimsical: fallout, the spread of radioactive particles after a nuclear blast, becomes "serendipitous," accidental, fortuitous discovery. Others are blatantly absurd: retaliation, the returning of like for like, becomes "anticipatory," occurring before, in advance. Some, finally, are simply obscene: a missile designed to carry between eight and fourteen indeptently targetable nuclear bombs is called a "peacekeeper."

Nuclear language limps, hobbles, and wobbles. It is language distorted. It becomes language standing on its head when we realize that it does exactly the opposite of what language is meant to do. Instead of communicating and revealing, *this* language hides things — deadly things. When one speaks of weapons systems with complex names such as air-launched cruise missiles or intermediate-range ballistic missiles, the use of acronyms is inevitable. Sometimes, however, these innocuous sounding abbreviations refer to deadly realities while they betray no hint of their devastating potentialities. A MARV might echo a nickname for someone named Marvin; it is a weapon which not only carries multiple nuclear bombs but will also "eventually have some degree of terminal, or final homing guidance built in so that as it approaches the target, it can make a last-minute maneuver to avoid a defensive interceptor and improve its final aim. . . . The *miss distance* at intercontinental range may become as little as thirty meters or less."[4] Experts talk about the "PK" of a weapons system; "PK" means the probability of kill. Perhaps there is only one acronym which conveys its real truth: the recent military strategy of mutual assured destruction is known as "MAD." The unending lists of acronyms hide the gruesome facts behind nuclear jargon and keep the average, non-scientific, non-military person from understanding what is really being said.

Nuclear language seems to take on a life of its own and all too frequently hides the truth even from those who use it and coin it. On November 17, 1985, the evening of the Geneva summit talks, the Detroit *Free Press* published an investigative article concerning the origins of the Strategic Defense Initiative. The article was fascinating in its portrayal of the secrets and maneuverings which led to the President's March 23, 1983 speech in which he announced plans for the SDI. According to the *Free Press,* Secretary of Defense Weinberger, although informed of the President's decision only four days in advance, backed the program completely. He apparently did not know a great deal about it, however. The following vignette graphically illustrates the penchant to use language to hide the truth.

But Weinberger was to make an unsettling discovery.

One day, as they headed toward a Star Wars congressional hearing, Weinberger had turned to DeLauer [Richard H. DeLauer, Undersecretary of Defense for Research and Engineering] and asked about the x-ray laser: "Is it a bomb?"

"I had to tell him," DeLauer recalled recently, "That's how you're going to get the x-ray. You're going to have to detonate a nuclear bomb in space."

Weinberger appeared disappointed. He repeated his question: 'It's not a bomb, is it?'

DeLauer, tactfully, said no, it would be a 'nuclear event.' "[5]

"Tactfully," a nuclear bomb becomes a nuclear "event." Dorothee Soelle is not alone in not wanting to see. She is, apparently, in the company of the U. S. Secretary of Defense.

The introduction of new terms which signify new distinctions also hides devastating new theories, such as the case with the distinction between "combatant" and "non-combatant." One of the absolutely fundamental tenets of "ethical" warfare has always been that massive numbers of innocent civilians must not be killed. The distinction was clear: one was military or civilian. Today, however, one hears more often about combatants and non-combatants. A member of the armed services is clearly a combatant, but so is anyone else even remotely involved or physically near. My recollection of an exchange between a prominent ethicist who has spent years formulating the ethics of nuclear war and the members of the Bishops' committee illustrates t tragic ramifications of this seemingly innocuous distinction

Committee member: I'm not sure I understand tinction clearly. Would a man working in, s plant, be a combatant?

Ethicist: Yes.

Committee member: What if his brought him his lunch? Would *he* be a

Ethicist: Yes.

Another committee member: T city. Within a ten mile radius o people. Would *they* be comba

Ethicist: Of course.

A change in terms, a new distinction, makes the death of millions — including little boys who take their fathers' lunches to them — "ethical."

The configuration of language expresses the nuclear reality, then distorts, reverses, and hides that very reality. This language contains technological terms which makes understanding nearly impossible for the non-specialist, and it encourages distinctions which in turn encourage massive destruction of cities and of persons. One cannot but wonder if some sort of terrible blasphemy is not present in such "naming."

Nuclear language is misleading and inadequate. Perhaps this is because it rises from a sexual bias. It is coined by men, used almost exclusively by men, and comes from a masculine world view. This bias, most often reflected in the abstract character of the language and its penchant to express theories and formulae, is often explicit, particularly when it relates to fear.

When defense budgets are in jeopardy, the spectre of defeat is always raised and the country (especially those who will vote on defense appropriations) is warned of the dire consequences of any cut in spending. The language — and the fears — are masculine. Our country, we are warned, will become "impotent." "We cannot allow our nation to become impotent in the face of he Soviet threat," we are told. Even more dreadful is the possibility of the "emasculation" of the American strength. Impoce and emasculation are masculine concerns, men's dreads.

A new image entered the language recently, one designed eate apprehension and consequently increased military ing. It is that of "the window of vulnerability." Any image erability genuinely frightens men. It suggests weakness, ity, and the feminine. Women are vulnerable, not men. e vulnerability is celebrated and exploited, whereas hidden and protected. There is an irony in this which e ignored: the weak remain exposed while the strong reater protection, and their protection is ineffective.

Mark Gerzon, in *A Choice of Heroes: The Changing Face of American Manhood,* reflects upon the paradox of protection and vulnerability as it is expressed in one of our national rituals, the TV football game.

> Covered with padding, crowned with helmets, bulging with muscles, and weighing over 200 pounds, the armored men will die sooner than the scantily clad cheerleaders dancing on the sidelines. Put the two figures side by side and they are diametric opposites: the woman exposed, her erogenous zones accentuated and (to the degree the law allows) revealed; the man encased, vulnerable parts of his body insulated against injury. Yet a few decades later, the ranks of the protected will have lost more members than the ranks of the exposed.[6]

Gerzon points to the paradox here: the least vulnerable are the most threatened. Being invulnerable does not mean being safe, yet the threat of an impotent, emasculated, vulnerable America creates more fear than does that of an annihilated America — at least for some of us. The inherited dominant masculine world view, including masculine fears, permeates nuclear language.

Logic

R. J. Lifton, referring to nuclear language, which he calls "a constellation of deception and self-deception that now dominates our world 'megamachine,' " says that it has "a strange rationality, 'the logic of madness.' "[7] Logic and reason have been held as central to human life for centuries. In our contemporary technological world they are subjects of idolatry, honored for their own sakes without any question as to their relationship to flesh and blood reality. The abstract is pure; it is seductive, it is escape; and in a nuclear world it is potentially terminal.

We have all learned that "Man is a rational animal," and that it is his capacity to reason which separates him from other animals. Every student learns the importance of logic and of clear reasoning. In our century, magnificent discoveries have been made in science, medicine, and technology. All of these are ultimately grounded in one's capacity to think, to reason, to move logically from one piece of data to the next. We formulate theories and test them, establish hypotheses and prove or disprove them. Science, physics, mathematics: these are the wonders of our time. They are fascinating and viewed as worthy of our most splendid efforts, our greatest minds, our enormous expenditures. Since the 1940s, this country has witnessed (and participated in) the growing importance of the science, scientists, logic and logicians of nuclear weapons and nuclear doctrines. Vast numbers of the people who are in important decision-making roles concerning both the development of weapons and their possible use reflect a mind-set which places rationality above all other considerations. One author, speaking of the "defense intellectuals" who are often called "the high priests of nuclear theology," describes the phenomenon:

> There is a foundation of faith buried beneath the intricate logic of their doctrines. Unlike other priesthoods, however, the "defense intellectuals" make logical reasoning not only the tool but the very content of their faith. Abstract, technical, mathematical reason is the god at whose throne they worship — though the Bomb seems to be seated at this god's right hand. The story of American nuclear policy is the story of their unbounded faith in the modern rational mind.[8]

Clearly, it is not this type of faith which requires a commitment to peacemaking, for even a cursory examination of such faith reveals a woefully inadequate response to the human condition. When one encounters the abstract theories and their bizarre consequences which flourish in policy-making areas, one is convinced of the truth of Lifton's phrase, "a logic of madness." The Theater of the Absurd has found a new home in the laboratories, offices, and board rooms of the "defense intellectuals."

Robert Scheer presents one scenario of this theater in his work, *With Enough Shovels: Reagan, Bush, and Nuclear War*.[9] Sheer gives an account of a prolonged interview with Thomas K. Jones, "the man Ronald Reagan had appointed Deputy Under Secretary for Defense for Research and Engineering, Strategic and Theater Nuclear Forces."[10] Jones had studied Soviet civilian defense manuals and believed that they showed that protection from nuclear bombs was easily attained. He maintained that the U. S. could recover from an all-out nuclear war with the Soviet Union in two to four years — *with shovels.*

According to Jones, a civil defense program similar to the Soviet Union's could enable most people (and machinery) to survive. While employed at Boeing, Jones performed tests to establish the effects of a nuclear blast on persons in shelters and on machinery buried in the ground. He became convinced that "90%" of the people would survive. All they would have to do is dig a shelter, cover it with wood, and cover that with dirt. "The dirt really is the thing that protects you from the blast as well as the radiation, *if there's radiation* [italics mine]. It protects you from the heat. You know, dirt is just great stuff."[11] Theater of the Absurd, the words of a raving lunatic? "Throughout the evening, Jones was scrupulously, indeed tediously, reasonable as he built his case that nuclear war was something far less terrible than I had been led to believe. . . ."[12]

T. K. Jones, while undoubtedly more vocal than most, is not unique. The Federal Emergency Management Agency (FEMA), charged with the nation's civil defense, maintains that 80 percent of the U. S. population would survive a nuclear war "if the bulk of the risk-area population had been evacuated to host areas prior to attack and if fallout protection had been developed and other crisis actions taken."[13] The agency does concede that there would indeed be great numbers of casualties, a grave lack of medical personnel and facilities. One of their handouts says that "people would have to help each other in an emergency," and recommends that "both adults and teenagers can acquire these valuable [First Aid] skills by taking free courses that are offered in many communities, such as a Red Cross First Aid course."[14]

Truly, these statements reflect a logic of madness. They bear no relation to either the national reality or the nuclear one. In a country where millions of citizens live in cities covered by cement and asphalt, the notion of people digging shelters and covering them with earth is ridiculous, particularly in terms of the poor who live in the overcrowded inner-city ghettos of our nation. One experience of any U. S. freeway at rush hour graphically demonstrates the impracticality of evacuation plans. Nuclear weapons which travel the globe in thirty minutes do not allow for long-term evacuations, and tourniquets and bandages will be useless in a nuclear war.

Such theories, while purporting to save lives, serve only to make nuclear war palatable, and they show a blatant disregard for human lives. FEMA says that 80 percent of the population would survive and 20 percent would perish; that is, almost 42 million men, women, and children would be killed. How, we must ask, can any "rational" person calmly accept the death of 42 million people? Such theories would be laughable except for one very important fact: they are not the work of some eccentric characters. They are the products of highly-financed studies done by influential members of the U. S. government. This makes them tragically frightening.

The "priests of reason" are not only in the government's bureaucracies, they are also in the scientific laboratories. Broad's study of the "Star Warriors" is particularly unsettling in this regard. He depicts a place and an atmosphere where the pursuit of science is uninhibited. The resources are magnificent, both in terms of budgets and scientific apparatus: "computer codes are played like a Wurlitzer organ."[15] One of the scientists describes life at the weapons lab: "There is a real aspect of debate here. Many of the interactions are thinly veiled aggressive displays. It's not just male society, it's a particularly self-selected variant of it. I used to call it 'ego war.' "[16]

These scientists, living in a "self-selected variant of the male society," are hard at work on the development of a third generation of nuclear weapons — the x-ray laser weapons of the SDI. While there is talk about the Soviet threat and even question as to the effectiveness of a defensive shield, the strongest sense that emerges from Broad's interviews is a fascination with the abstract, the theory. Comments by two members of the group are particularly revealing and somehow very sad. Larry West, who maintains that he is not working on weapons of death but "weapons of life," says: "I didn't want to be known as a weapons designer . . . I still don't. I want to be known for doing something much more significant for society. On the other hand, I'm very interested in designing weapons because I believe in being able to defend the country. Also, I find the problems fascinating."

Larry discusses his introduction to the study of science:

> I loved it. . . . It was a treat. I had emotional problems at home with my family life and my mother. Science was a world that was pure and no longer had emotions. It would never go away and would never leave you. And it was always correct. There was always a right answer. So it had a strong attraction for me emotionally. On top of that I had a knack for it.[17]

Peter Hagelstein describes his first impression of the Livermore laboratory. In 1975 he was twenty years old, a student in the graduate school of the Massachusetts Institute of Technology, and on his way to a summer job at Livermore.

The lab itself made quite an impression . . . especially the guards and barbed wire. When I got to the personnel department it dawned on me that they worked on weapons here, and that's about the first I knew about it. I came pretty close to leaving. I didn't want to have anything to do with it. Anyway, I met nice people, so I stayed. The people were extremely interesting. And I really didn't have anywhere else to go.[18]

Peter's views changed over the years. "Until 1980 or so I didn't want to have anything to do with nuclear anything. Back in those days I thought there was something fundamentally evil about weapons. Now I see it as an interesting physics problem."[19]

These young men exemplify the rationalistic abstractionism which underlies so much of the discussion, planning, and policy-making in the nuclear world. Equations and computers, "always a right answer," "interesting problems," these describe a sadly limited life, yet one highly valued and intensely encouraged in the male-dominated world. Broad's conclusion is telling:

The young scientists have never seen the sky painted with the reds and oranges of a high-altitude nuclear explosion. They have never felt the flash of heat from a distant nuclear blast. They are creating a world of nuclear weapons they can know only through the sanitized flicker of electronic meters and the painstaking analysis of chart paper.

High-tech Gulags such as O group [group name for the scientists] are seductive. They push science and technology to the limit and impose none of the terrible physical privations of their Soviet counterparts. But in some respects they may be more insidious. The

prisoners are there of their own accord, serving both
science and war, creating in order to destroy, part of
an elite, yet pawns in a terrifying game.[20]

Even as the most protected are the most vulnerable, so too,
the priests of reason become reason's sacrifices. The game is terrifying, yet men aren't supposed to show fear. Much has been
written recently concerning the suppression of emotions in the
male world. We all know that "grown men don't cry," and that a
public display of feelings is a definite sign of weakness. The John
Wayne image, the strong, brave, silent, unemotional hero who
is always in control has profoundly affected and afflicted generations of American men and women. If one were to doubt that
this image still prevails, one has only to view the official portrait
of President Reagan that hangs in the Presidents' room of the
National Portrait Gallery in Washington, D. C. He is dressed in
jeans, hands in back pockets, boots suitably scuffed, belt buckle
appropriately elaborate.

R. J. Lifton reports the terrible struggles Vietnam veterans
have had in coming to grips with this image and in moving
beyond it.[21] One young man, recounting his feelings after killing
a Vietcong soldier with a knife, "added rather softly: 'I felt sorry.
I don't know why I felt sorry. John Wayne never felt sorry.' "[22]
Gerzon echoes this when he quotes Frank Barber, a Vietnam
veteran who suffered a mental breakdown when he returned to
the U.S. "The Navy gave him medals. But what he really
needed, he said, was to be held and comforted by his wife. Why
couldn't he ask his own wife for solace? 'I never saw John Wayne
walk up to a woman and say,'I need a hug.' "[23]

The ideal of the controlled, rational man is not limited to
soldiering. It affects all areas of one's life. Gerzon reflects upon
the difficulty men face when owning their feelings. When he and
his wife experience tension in their relationship, she will often
say, "Why can't you be more open about your feelings?" He continues:

> How can I explain it to her? How can any man explain it to any woman? Women are not raised to abort all tears. They are not measured by their toughness. They are not expected to bang against each other on hockey rinks and football fields and basketball courts. They do not go out into the woods to play soldiers. They do not settle disagreements by punching each other. For them, tears are a badge of femininity. For us, they are a masculine demerit.[24]

The "demerit" of acknowledged emotions is alive and well in the nuclear issue. Feelings have nothing to do with abstract theory, nor with interesting physics problems. Emotions have no place at the tables where policy issues are discussed nor in rooms where targeting doctrines are put into effect and nuclear bombs are aimed at people. The psychic numbing endemic to our times finds an easy foothold among those who already deny emotion. Yet, those who deny feelings also deny psychic numbing. Rational people are neither emotional (sentimental, hysterical, feminine), nor are they numb. They are reasonable and logical. Joanna Rogers Macy quotes a fascinating and chilling statement in this regard. William G. Hyland, former Deputy Director of the National Security Council, said, "Psychic numbing does not exist at the top levels of government. Of course, if you allow the emotion of nuclear war to enter the Defense Department, you'd end up totally paralyzed."[25]

Within the world of nuclear weapons, then, emotions are suspect. They are signs of inferiority, of incapacity to really understand the issues. Those who show emotion are perceived as incapable of authentic discussion on nuclear issues. Gerzon quotes the response of a former colleague of Daniel Ellsberg's from the RAND corporation who had heard Ellsberg deliver a speech. "The Dan Ellsberg I used to know was analytical, factual, sober, informative. The man I heard today was emotional, irrational, with no relation to reason or argument."[26] Ellsberg's emotions destroyed his credibility.

Nowhere is the dismissal of emotions more effective than in response to the peace movement. Members of the peace movement are dismissed as "hysterical," or are charged with using emotion as a means of misleading and manipulating the public. On May 9, 1982, the *Washington Post* published a memo the U.S. Arms Control and Disarmament Agency sent to the White House outlining a media campaign to counteract the publicity of Ground Zero Week (a series of teach-ins, etc. organized by the Ground Zero organization). The memo is amazing and would be laughable were it not that its source was the government agency charged with arms control and disarmament. It is *very* revelatory of this agency's view of emotion in the peace movement.

"The press and electronic media will be full of demagoguery and emotion as journalists hungrily interview tearful mothers and self-righteously indignant clergymen against a mushroom cloud background," the memo says. A plan is then presented for government response for each day of the week, beginning with "Ground Zero Week, minus one." That day, the memo suggests, a photo opportunity should be arranged: "President and Mrs. Reagan at Camp David: spring flowers — atmosphere of calm." On day three there is to be a "Fireside chat" by the President on peace with "(no hardware or balance discussions)." Day five will have "Kennedy demagoguery," and so the *Wall Street Journal* should have an editorial about "hysteria and policy development — the need for calm . . ." Ground Zero week plus one provides a scenario: "Ground Zero Week closing remarks in Lafayettte Park — much sound and fury (White House backdrop)."[27] While this plan was not carried out, its very formulation demonstrates a mockery of emotion ("tearful mothers"), a connection of them with sinister practices ("full of demagoguery and emotion"), and most significantly of all, the sense that this emotion-laden peace movement is a serious threat.

The male mistrust of emotions and the conviction that serious people do not voice their fears found its way into the Bishops' pastoral on war and peace. In the opening paragraphs of the pastoral, the Bishops speak of the terror in the minds and hearts of their people, and say they share it. Yet, in paragraph 132, the Bishops refer to the committee's consultations with those responsible for the country's nuclear strategy and those opposed to it. "It has been a sobering and perplexing experience," the text says.[28] The draft text said, "It has been a sobering, perplexing, and, at times, *frightening* experience" [italics mine]. The word "frightening" was removed from the text, even though the experience was indeed a fearsome one for many. There was no long discussion about this change; in fact, it seemed natural. Perhaps that's even more telling.

The cult of the rational, of provable facts, of elaborate theory, of logic, combined with a profound mistrust of emotion is not a new phenomenon. It has been an essential aspect of the male ethos for centuries.[29] What is *new* is the risk involved today. That risk is every thing and every one. The logic of madness is mad; it is, as one former Secretary of Defense agreed, "the rationalization of insanity." Yet it continues, its powerful influence still holds sway. I believe it does so because it is powerful — and power is really the heart of the matter.

Power

In January, 1986, a new film was released. Its title was "Power," and the advertisements declared: "More seductive than sex . . . More addictive than any drug . . . More precious than gold . . . Power. Nothing else comes close." Perhaps no word is so ambiguous as "power," and no concept quite so seductive. Everyone, it would seem, wants power. No one is sure, however, what power is nor how it best functions. Webster's Unabridged Dictionary lists sixteen definitions for "power," ranging from "ability to do, capacity to act;" to "ability to control others; authority; sway; influence;" to "an armed force; army; navy [archaic]."[30] In his extensive study of power and innocence, Rollo May defines power as "the ability to cause or prevent change." He then discusses at length what he views as five kinds of power which range from "exploitative" to "integrative."[31]

While the many definitions of power vary, they all contain two common elements: energy and movement. Power, whether it be electric, atomic, brain-power, or brute-power, implies an energy, a certain vitality which leads to some kind of movement, either abrupt as in an explosion or more subtle as in the flow of electricity. Power, then, does not seem to be so much a "thing" which one possesses as it is a strength, a capacity into which one enters, with which one cooperates, by which — at times — one is overcome or destroyed.

The energy of power is not a static entity but rather one which functions, which *does* something. One need only witness the energy of a thunderstorm, the devastation of an earthquake, the majesty of an erupting volcano to know the awesome, fearsome functioning of power. At the same time, the steady flow of a river, a flow which can create huge caverns and miles-long canyons, speaks of the relentless quality of power. Like all energy, power can function for life or for death.

Never before in history has humankind possessed the capacity to unleash power as it does today. Whether or not that will happen depends to a great extent upon the ways in which the powerful view power, especially when faced with conflict. How does power work among the superpowers? What and where is power in the United States?

Whether or not the devastating power of nuclear weapons is unleashed in our world depends a great deal on other, accepted understandings of power as it functions in life. Decisions about the use of nuclear weapons will not be arrived at by a process which is somehow different from that by which other decisions are made. Views of nuclear power are profoundly related to views of any power. History shows us a continuous tendency to equate power with domination and with the ability to control others. American history reflects the pattern of a dominant group (white male) which, imbued with a sense of destiny, pushes forward and upward, shaping the future of the nation. In order to shape this future, however, it was deemed necessary to either eliminate or control those groups which stood in the way of its accomplishment. As we have seen, genocide and slavery were part of that process, as were devastation of the land, control of education, limited voting rights, and a double standard of ethical conduct.

Power in this context is what Joanna Rogers Macy calls a "zero-sum game."[32] There is only so much power and if you have it, I don't. Worse, if you want some, I'll have to give up some of mine. Only a few can have power and those few must protect it from the rest. If power is control, then your power implies that you will control me. Such an idea is obviously frightening to the ones "in power." One need only recall the fear and strong sense of the ominous which permeated the white community when terms like "black power" entered the nation's vocabulary. Would black power mean the end of white power? Will "giving" power to women mean that men won't have any anymore?

Zero-sum, patriarchal power functions in as many ways as there are men and women who live by it. There are, however, three characteristics of such power which are generally present and which have profound ramifications in the area of war and peace. This power seeks to control and to dominate and it does so by relying heavily on secrecy. It is further marked by an intense rigidity; and, finally, it equates power with strength and with force.

The tales and images of secrecy are myriad: the "power-brokers" in the stereotypical backroom at a political convention, the inside tips of the knowledgeable who have information about the latest corporate merger, the back booth in a restaurant where the "boss" decides who will live and who will die, the confidential "eyes only" document. All of these images presuppose a valuing of secrecy and a reluctance to share information. Knowledge becomes power and, again, power must not be shared. As power, knowledge is used to manipulate people. Information is "leaked" in order to make a political point. The need for secrecy is used as justification for actions which are deemed questionable. The refusal to allow the news media access to Granada at the time of the U.S. invasion remains a classic example of such manipulation.

The secrecy which surround the spectrum of nuclear weapons and nuclear policy is legendary. The first atomic weapons were built in secrecy, the decision to use them was made in secrecy, their locations, numbers, destructive potential are cloaked in secrecy. Only a select few know the real truth about the nuclear arsenal; therefore, only this few are capable of correct decisions. The elaborate measures taken to protect this information witness to a need to control by secrecy and to the futility of such attempts. Classified documents multiply, but so too the number of persons who have access to them. Periodic calls for lie detector tests of government employees are issued; intelligence agencies grow larger and more powerful. At the same time, the number of spies increases and the information sold to others becomes more sensitive. Millions of dollars, untold amounts of creative energy and unimaginable hours of concerned investigation are devoted to the project of keeping our secrets safe from the enemy, of controlling information. A great irony is involved in all of this. A preoccupation with secrecy is grounded upon an obsession with security, and yet the secrets are those which keep the world in the most terrifying insecurity it has ever known.

While secrecy is based upon the need to be secure from the enemy who would use the knowledge to destroy us, it is all too often used against us. The citizens become the enemy. White trains carrying nuclear weapons travel the country in secrecy, top government officials are kept in the dark about major decisions, military budgets are ambiguous, and those who inform people about questionable practices are suspected of treason. When secrecy is pivotal to power, it displays a disturbing tendency to transform itself into paranoia.

Power as control necessarily implies a rigidity which is manifested in an inability to tolerate dissent and an aversion to self-examination. The mirror of conversion, so necessary for the making of peace, is not very popular among those for whom power is domination. For such persons, ideas which question the *status quo* are dangerous ideas. The persons who propose them are ttreated with suspicion. From the time of J. Edgar Hoover until today, there have been ample and disheartening examples of the tendency to view dissenters as either naive or "soft on communism." Robert Oppenheimer, one of the "fathers" of the atomic bomb, lost his security clearance when he began to question the escalation of the arms race. Albert Einstein's character was questioned when he began to speak out against the same race. Martin Luther King Jr.'s phones were tapped, his character viciously maligned when he, too, spoke out. Today the offices of peace activists are invaded, their movements are monitored.

One of the most common methods of dealing with dissent within this context is that of questioning the loyalty of the dissenter. Those who do not follow accepted lines of thought or who speak out against governmental policies are portrayed as disloyal and as working for the downfall of the nation. They must be watched, and those who are close to them must also be watched.

The stress on loyalty and the extremes to which some will go to assure that loyalty (unquestioning obedience), were brought home to me in a personal way a few years ago. One of my nephews, a bright, articulate, independent person, became interested in working in the diplomatic corps. After several series of interviews and several batteries of tests, he met with a member of the State Department for what was to be his final interview — by his choice. He was asked if he could be loyal, if he could uphold and support the policies of his government — given who his aunt was. The U.S. Department of State knew who I was, knew of my work on the Bishops' committee and was concerned about the loyalty of my nephew! Once again the ridiculous and the ominous coincide.

While the obsession with secrecy and loyalty is irritating and sometimes dangerous, the inability of zero-sum power to sustain any self-examination is tragic. Self-examination demands that we hear other voices and other opinions; it also implies an openness to change. Change, however, always implies a redistribution of power. If power is limited, if I have a lot of it, if I fear losing it, I will necessarily spend energy in keeping it. Growth and development are sacrificed as life becomes an impossible struggle to preserve power, and this burden can be overwhelming. How can one live if one can never be wrong?

Such a burden is personally devastating, but it becomes communally life-threatening when it is part of the decision-making of a nation. How can people hope for a safer world when its most powerful members refuse to question the process which has brought them to such danger? When the Bishops' committee met with members of the State Department, I found myself asking this question over and over.

Everyone around the table in the State Department conference room agreed that we all wanted peace. What we disagreed about was the proper means of achieving that peace. When members of the committee appeared to question the Administration's choice of means, the men who represented the State Department tried first to indicate that the Bishops didn't really know whereof they spoke. They then became angry. The bombing of Hiroshima and Nagasaki entered the discussion within the context of the country's particular obligation to work for peace and its particular responsibility for arms control. At that point, the Undersecretary of State for Political Affairs asked if the committee meant to imply that there was something wrong with the U. S. actions in Hiroshima and Nagasaki. When some people nodded their heads, the Undersecretary pounded his fist on the table and declared (shouted, really): "Then we have nothing more to talk about!" The suggestion that our country might have done something wrong provoked a violent reaction which effectively ended any possibility for mutual understanding or collaboration.

That violent reaction reflected another aspect of power in the male-dominated world. It is synonymous with a strength most often measured in terms of force. Power which functions as control must be able to overpower that which threatens it. The intimate connection between physical force and common understandings of power is undeniable. If I cannot convince or dismiss my opponent, then I must be able to force him or her to do my will. I must overcome. Power becomes brute-power.

This power, personified for us in characters such as Rambo and Rocky, or celebrities such as wrestlers, football players or mighty avengers who say things like "Make my day," who are held up for the American culture as heroes by the President of this country, readily resort to violence to have their way. In so doing, they legitimize violence and connect it with winning, with being a hero, with being a man. One man quoted in *A Choice of Heroes* reflects on the meaning of such violence. Tom Mosmiller works at a shelter for battered women and children. He counsels the men who do the battering. He is committed to working to end violence.

> Before getting involved with the men's movement, I spent several years as an antiwar activist. I was opposed to the way America tried to throw its weight around in the world. Finally, I saw the problem was deeper than foreign policy. It was a problem of men. We were not only violent in Vietnam. We were violent in the way we use the earth, violent in the way we make energy, violent in the way we play games, even violent in our own homes. We are violent in almost every thing we do.[33]

Patriarchal power, which is power by domination, not only legitimizes violence, it encourages it. It is not surprising that the greatest symbol of power in our world is also the most violent. The U.S. and the U.S.S.R. are "superpowers" because they possess vast arsenals of the most destructive, most violent weapons the world has ever known. They are, further, locked into a deadly race to have more and more of that power which can already destroy the earth. A nuclear bomb is a perfect paradigm. Those who have it have strength; they can force others to do their will (or at least others who do not have the bomb). It is our defense against those who would seek to over-power us. It presupposes a world view in which those who dis-agree with us are indeed a threat to us. A nuclear bomb brooks no argument, allows for no discussion. It is mighty. And it is futile. The superpowers have created something which has overpowered them and which holds them captive. A recent pro-duction of the Second City Theater in Chicago, "How Green Were My Values," had a skit in it which expressed the futility and absurdity of nuclear weapons most graphically. "The Rus-sians have a new weapon." "What does it do?" "Nothing." "Then what can we do?" "Nothing." "Those bastards!!"

Relationship

Power as domination is often translated into the dynamics of that which is fundamental to human life — relationships. All too often our ways of relating with one another are in fact struggles for power, efforts to dominate each other. Within a society which is structured according to the givens of male dominance, mas-culine "virtues" prevail. As this is true in the cult of rationality and the manifestations of power, so too it is reflected in both the structure and the dynamic of human relationship. Almost all forms of relationships are hierarchical, in practice if not in theory. One person/group is the determiner within the relation-ship and others function in response to the determiner. If one were to diagram such relationships, the form would be that of a pyramid, with the largest numbers also being the lowest layers. The majority form the base and support the other layers; they are *beneath* and controlled by what is above them.

The person "on top" makes the decisions, imposes his will upon the others. In the traditional marriage, for example, the

husband/father chooses where/how the family will live. The
wife, the helpmate or "little woman" must comply with the husband's decisions — at least overtly. If she does not, she faces
bleak prospects such as poverty if she leaves the marriage or violence if she stays within it. This same pattern repeats itself in
our larger, societal relationships. The corporation is kept alive
by those who struggle up through the various levels in order to
reach the top. Those who question the decisions, policies, or
ethics of a corporation can either leave it, hide their questions,
or remain frozen at a lower level. Churches have rigid hierarchical models. The vast majority of their members are not the ones
who make decisions, who articulate belief in contemporary contexts, who fashion the churches' response to today's challenges.
Those who dissent do not suffer physical violence, perhaps, but
their souls are often battered beyond recognition.

Although the leaders of our government are chosen by their
constituencies, the functioning of the government is frequently
characterized by power struggles. The sad spectacle of the various maneuverings for influence which have dominated the
Reagan White House staff give witness to relationships which
are not founded upon a common goal or shared vision but rather
on individuals who seek to have the most power. While our system of government has built-in balances which help prevent a
totalitarian or despotic use of power, the military does not. The
military represents hierarchical, power-based relationship at
its most blatant. One is trained to obey orders without question,
to carry out the orders of superior officers completely and with
enthusiasm. One is also trained to violence, always reminded
that one must be ready to attack and to kill the enemy.

As the relational structure of a military organization is
hierarchy and coercive power *par excellence,* it is also male *par
excellence.* There are women in the military and some have attained high officer status. Their presence has not, however, affected the male model in any significant way. Their very presence is questioned, particularly in areas where "real" soldiers

function: the battlefield, the training camps, and, most recently, the military academies. Assistant Secretary of Defense James Webb was recently featured in an article in the *Washington Post*. In a speech to the U.S. Naval Academy (which admits women students), Webb talks about what Marines are saying about the Naval academy graduates. "(To be honest, the reaction is mixed. They will tell you that you are the only academy officers not indoctrinated in an all-male environment.)" The article continues: " 'The original purpose of a tough plebe indoctrination was to filter out people who can't handle stress,' Webb says, as he spins out his thesis that the admission of women in 1976 forced a new emphasis on academics over a punishing physical and psychological regime. 'This,' he says, 'is no way to build leaders.' " Webb wrote a magazine article, "Women Can't Fight," in order to fight the idea of women in combat. His reasons are revelatory: "He asserted that women were innately less violent: 'Women don't rape men, and it has nothing to do, obviously, with socially-induced differences. . . . Furthermore, men fight better without women around.' "[34]

"The single greatest difference between men and women, other than the obvious biological differences, is that the male must win the title of 'man' by becoming a potential killer, while women retain the luxury of innocence," writes Sam Keen.[35] Gerzon would agree; for he maintains that the soldier is *the* role model for the American male. From childhood on, males are trained to soldier. The characteristics and the personality traits which make for good soldiers are also those which are most valued for men. Historically, it has been the soldier who had defended the country, saved the lives of loved ones with his bravery and heroism. He has been the hero in virtually every cultural system, "because without him, that system could not endure."

> To embody courage under the most gruesome circumstances, the Soldier had to repress his fear. To embody strength, he had to repress his sensitivity. To

kill, he had to repress compassion. No alternative
existed. So men through the ages have measured
themselves against what seemed to be male destiny.
Rather than deny it, we have embraced it. Those who
have not, we called cowards. What war required was,
by definition, manliness. The men who were the best
soldiers were, in effect, the best men.[36]

A boy becomes a man in the military. In so doing, his capacity for violence is unleashed, his brutality praised, his tenderness berated (the worst epithet — "a woman"), his fear suppressed, his creativity denied. His relationships are those of
shared force and violence, slavish obedience, physical violence
against an enemy. Patriarchal power thrives in this context,
and — because it is the model for manhood — influences all aspects of American culture. While not every little boy grows up to
be a soldier, every little boy is affected by the soldier image. And
so is every little girl, for she, too, grows up in a world shaped by
that image — a world which degrades her own qualities. "In the
patriarchical tradition, which has created the warrior psyche,
both the female and the feminine virtues have been degraded.
Women and all things feminine must be kept in control."[37]

Language, logic, power, and relationship, all profoundly affected and colored by a masculine world view are, as I have said,
inadequate for the crisis of our time. They not only endure, however, they intensify. As they intensify, they also terrify those
who look to the future. Nowhere does the insidious confluence of
these patterns portend more danger than in the functioning of
the world's most important relationship: that between enemies.

I am aware of the fact that I have not yet responded to what
is inevitably someone's first questions when the issues of war
and peace are raised: "But what about the Soviets?" I have re-
frained from doing so until now for two reasons. The first is that
this book is primarily an attempt to speak from my own experiences and from the searching for directions which those experi-

ences provoked in me and in so many others with whom I have spoken, worried, prayed, and hoped. My questions concern not so much the conversion of the communists as they do our own conversion. The mirror into which the peacemaker must look reflects her/his own image, not that of the "enemy." One's own failures cannot be laid at the feet of another's sins. While it may be a natural tendency to say that "the devil made me do it," such reasoning is neither accurate nor honest. The repeated use of the question about the Soviets has led me to wonder not about the Soviets but about us.

Secondly, it is vitally important to ask that question within its correct context. For me, that context is one of how we relate to others, especialy others who disagree with us, who threaten us, whose power presents a real or perceived danger to us. The relationships between the two world superpowers represent an extreme, but very real, example of how unexamined modes of thought and action lead to dead and deadly ends.

The first atomic bomb was built in terms of an enemy; it was used against a different enemy. The hydrogen bomb was created to stay ahead of a third enemy, and all weapons systems since then have been justified by the enemy's weapons. If there were no enemy, there would be no reason for these horrible weapons. At times, one is led to ask which is more important, the enemy or the weapons? The enemy as such is profoundly significant for us; its existence enables us to justify ways of acting and thinking that would otherwise be unconscionable. The enemy is our excuse.

Each time the Bishops' committee spoke with an expert who either represented or promoted the present Administration's policy of military escalation, a certain pattern of argument would appear. The President (or, we, the administration, the State Department, the Department of Defense, etc.) wants peace. *But,* the Soviets are so evil. *Therefore,* we must build more weapons (or, be prepared to destroy them, make our defense systems impregnable, never trust them, etc.)

Enemies are projections of our own dark side, and the language we use to speak of them reflects the denial of our own evil. This language is laden with emotion and exaggeration. It is filled with lies. Such language hides the reality of human beings, it reduces them to stereotypes, subhuman monsters. "The Soviets are Godless communists," we are told, and they seek to build an "evil empire." They are "worse than Hitler," according to one member of the State Department; and "all they do is lie," according to a chief U.S. arms negotiator. When we rob someone of their reality, when we reduce a nation of men, women, and children to a stereotype, then we can destroy it. The "Japs" in World War II, the "gooks" in Vietnam, the "commies" today: "Wipe 'em out!"

The system of government, the stated values of a democracy, the common hopes of the people of free countries are all clearly in disagreement with the governmental system and philosophy of the leadership of the Soviet Union. Very few would argue this. Even fewer would not find the policies and actions of those same leaders questionable. Soviet leaders have put enormous energy into building their own arsenals of nuclear weapons. They have denied freedom to their own citizens and taken away the freedom of other nations. They do challenge — actively — the leadership of the U.S. within the global community. They cannot be ignored.

The pattern of dealing with them — and with all conflict — is one which springs from a patriarchical model of power and of relationship. Conflict must be controlled, suppressed, or denied. But we cannot control, suppress, or deny the Soviet Union. And so the force and struggle for domination escalates until we are able to destroy them. But to destroy them is to destroy ourselves. And on it goes. As long as any partner in a conflictual relationship is reduced to the "enemy," as long as relationships are primarily power struggles, as long as power is equated with force and violence, there can be no way out of the terror.

Within this chapter, I have sought to reflect upon the sources of the world's terror as they are related to a male-dominated ethos. I have also tried to show the profound relationship between nuclear terror and the way we talk and think, the way we feel about power, and how we relate to one another. The arduous commitment to peacemaking is made all the more arduous because it calls for conversion in all these areas of our lives.

The commitment is one all of us must make. While the preceding pages speak of the masculine reality, they are not meant to imply that the feminine is not involved. Little girls do grow up in the shadow of the soldier image, and they are led to encourage it. Women do sometimes opt for coercive, manipulative power. We all know this. Nonetheless, the model remains the masculine one, and the feminine is absent from places and conversations wherein men make decisions about the world's future. Women's voices are not heard, their "instincts" are devalued. During the entire course of the Bishops' committee's meetings, which lasted almost two years and included dozens of meetings and involved numerous experts, only three women spoke to the committee. One was a scripture scholar, two were peace activists. In all of our meetings with departments of the government, the only other women I ever saw were receptionists, secretaries, and cleaning women. I often felt lonely and alienated. I slowly began to realize that this was not simply because I was "the only woman," but rather because as the only woman, I was very much alone in a world view, a relationship to reality. Sexism is an evil. Nowhere is it more evil than in making of war.

Any questions which I had concerning the connection between the arms race and sexism were resolved for me by some pictures I saw of three women. In the winter of 1982, I attended a seminar for Church leaders sponsored by the Center for Defense Information in Washington, D.C. One session was devoted to the yearly Arms Bazaars. The speaker showed the group a series of slides which had been surreptitiously taken at the same recent Bazaar. One of those slides showed a woman, dressed in cowboy hat, shorts, and a fringed leather halter top, running a roulette wheel for the enjoyment of prospective purchasers of weapons. Two other slides also showed women, both of whom wore bikinis. One was seated straddling a missile. The other was reclining on top of one.

Is there no way out of the terror? Are there no alternatives, no other images? Chapter Four addresses these questions.

4
"Poor Old War God Losing Power"
NEW PATTERNS

The image of women adorning death machines and of men ogling both weapons and women evokes something ugly and shameful in all of us. It also speaks more eloquently than any words about what is so degrading in a male-dominated world galloping toward death. Women and weapons are sexy. They are desirable objects which men seek to own, possess, overcome. Little wonder most women feel an instinctive revulsion towards weapons; their "instinct" in many ways is one of self-preservation.

There are other images, however, *and* other women and men. Their faces reflected in the mirror of our common humanity offer us hope in what we could become. They show us ways to counter and to heal the terror. One such image, an extremely powerful one, is that of the Mothers of the Plaza de Mayo in Buenos Aires, Argentina.

> Many of them are well-dressed, in tweeds or expensive sweaters; not at all the kind of women who normally appear at demonstrations. Others have the brown complexions and broad faces that show their Indian origins; they come perhaps from the provinces

bordering on Paraguay or Brazil. But the majority
are unremarkable in their appearance, wearing
heavy-heeled flat shoes and sensible clothes, and the
white scarves which have become their symbol.[1]

These women, and thousands like them, have gathered
each week in silent demonstration of their search for lost loved
ones. They have come together to demand the truth about those
who have been taken from them. Their pain drew them together, and their courage kept them together. Powerless, often
poor, threatened themselves with disappearance, their continuing presence denied terror its ultimate victory.

But the name of the square where the tear gas and
vomit gas once billowed out to envelop them, and
where the riot police weighed in with their heavy
night-sticks to beat them about the head and kid-
neys, is now identified firmly with the Mothers, not
with their tormentors. They outlasted the men in the
Casa Rosada who set the police on them.[2]

It is a woman such as this that Isabel Allende describes so
movingly in *The House of the Spirits*. Thrown out on the ground
in the middle of the night by those who had captured and tor-
tured her, the narrator describes the woman who brought her
into her home.

A short dark woman came out to meet me. Her legs
were crossed with veins and her eyes were sunk in a
web of generous wrinkles that did not make her look
old. She smiled, and I saw that some of her teeth were
missing. She came up to me and straightened the
blanket with a brusque, timid gesture that took the
place of the hug she was afraid to give me.

"I'm going to give you a little cup of tea. I don't
have any sugar, but something warm will do you

good," she said.

We stayed up all night talking. She was one of those stoical, practical women of our country, the kind of woman who has a child with every man who passes through her life and, on top of that, takes in other people's abandoned children, her own poor relatives, and anybody else who needs a mother, a sister, or an aunt; the kind of woman who's the pillar of many other lives, who raises her children to grow up and leave her and lets her men leave too, without a word of reproach, because she has more pressing things to worry about. She looked like so many others I had met in the soup kitchens, in my Uncle Jaime's clinic, at the church office where they would go for information on their disappeared, and in the morgue where they would go to find their dead. I told her she had run an enormous risk rescuing me, and she smiled. It was then I understood that the days of Colonel Garcia and all those like him are numbered, because they have not been able to destroy the spirit of these women.[3]

These women, whose spirits cannot be destroyed, whose courage is of the enduring sort, whose caring is so very human, these women, and the men who accompany them, are the hope of our age. They are present, they will not go away. They make the hidden public in their refusal to cloak their grieving. They will not be silent and in their speaking the disappeared are given voice.

There are many new voices among us these days. Some are strident and angry, others are sorrowful and filled with grief, still others are hopeful and confident. These new voices are saying new things and old things in new ways. They're suggesting, questioning, demanding. They call for change and transformation, alternative visions and new patterns of life. They're different, these voices; they're exciting and threatening. They're women's voices.

Women's voices have been stifled for centuries — even to themselves. They've been limited to certain tones, specific vocabularies, "appropriate" subjects, and private places. Now, however, they're speaking out, and what they have to say is crucial to the planet's survival. Women everywhere have begun to own their experience and to value their importance. Alternative experiences have suggested alternative approaches. Different voices pose new problems; they also articulate new solutions.

All areas of public and private life have been affected by the raising of women's voices and women's consciousness. For some that's good news; for others it's unmitigated disaster, or at least *her*esy. Either way, the voices won't be silenced. One of the areas where they are raised with greatest urgency is that of nuclear terror. They're shouting at Greenham Common and singing in New York. They're chanting in Washington, questioning in Bonn, and praying in Los Angeles. What are these women saying and why? More importantly, does what they say offer any hope for us and for our world?

A massive amount of work has been done in the past twenty years concerning women's experience, women's moral development, feminine psychology, and women's spirituality. The stories and studies, the books and plays, the art exhibits and poetry and music are fascinating, enriching, enraging, amazing — and *important*. They reveal a world unique from, yet deeply immersed in, the "real" (i.e. male) world. They uncover alternative world views and provide significant ways of healing the terrible, terrorizing sickness of our time. If we return to the four areas of language, logic, power, and relationship and view them in terms of women's experience, we will, I believe, find much to think about, to integrate, to activate. We may even discover ways to peace.

Language

Nothing has provoked more controversy recently than the question of "the so-called common language."[4] All of us know the horror stories: people enraged at the thought of changing even one word, others dismissing the subject as frivolous or insignificant, still others claiming fidelity to the "purity" of language, continuing to use sexist vocabulary. All of us also know the rage, the frustration, the despair sometimes, of those who feel themselves to be ignored, demeaned, and insulted. Emotion runs strong in the language debate and visceral reactions tend to be the norm. These very reactions reveal the importance of language even as many deny it. To change language is to change the world view expressed therein; it is a fundamental and radical shift in perspective *and* in values. "The so-called common language" is no longer.

Language as disclosure has taken on new significance with the advent of the women's movement. This fact is vitally important in relation to nuclear terror. A people's language, as we have seen, can serve to reveal or to hide. It can name truly or it can belie the reality. Language enables communication or denies it. Words praise or condemn; they are worship or blasphemy; they are truth or lies.

Women's rising consciousness has recognized the pervasive and nearly universal use of language to make one half of the world invisible. If someone came to America from a distant place and listened to the public pronouncements, the official statements, the churches' worship services, she or he would logically conclude that all the people they saw walking around were men. Women simply do not exist in much of our language. All men, after all, were created equal, and all men were redeemed. Mankind has evolved to this point in time and everyone knows the importance of one man, one vote. The lawyer, he, the doctor, he, the executive, he, and the priest, he, all belong to the same brotherhood and share fellowship. The brethren pray to Him, while the working man earns his daily bread.

One could go on forever with this kind of language, much of
the world would love to. Women, however, have begun to refuse
to remain invisible. They insist that they are no one's brother
and that God has redeemed women too. The lawyer, she, the doctor, she, the executive, she, and even, in some traditions, the
priest, she, all share the same sisterhood today, and they will no
longer be hidden under the rubric of "brotherhood." As long as
any group remains hidden it can be ignored and the injustices
perpetrated against it continue unimpeded. If there were no
Mothers of the Plaza, the disappeared would go unnoticed.

The move from sexist to inclusive language is a difficult one.
It requires major rethinking and great creativity. It also requires the recognition of the truth of women's place in society
and in church. The tragic explosion of the Challenger space
shuttle in January, 1986, showed the contradictions of sexist
language — as well as the difficulty in getting beyond such language — in a particularly poignant way. The loss of the crew of
the Challenger was felt with a specially intense sorrow because
its members represented the marvelous diversity of our country: black, white, oriental, male, female. In addition, Christa
McAuliffe, bright and shining school teacher, touched America's
heart in special ways. She was like us as we would like to be.
And she was going out in space, and she was killed. We grieved,
not only for her, I suspect, but also for something inside each of
us.

All of the commentators and commentaries were particularly sensitive to this unique dimension in the country's sorrow.
They also had problems with language. The most visible
member of the crew was a wonderful woman — not an as-
tronaut, but a teacher. Her very presence on the mission became
a major issue in the inevitable questions after the fact. The difficulties many commentators had in posing the question,
"Should *she* be part of *manned* space flights?" were obvious and,
I am sure, discomfiting for many. The invisible becomes visible
and the language is inadequate.

Women, knowing first-hand the effects of being made invisible, are particularly sensitive to whatever else is hidden in language. Expressions like collateral damage, countervalue, peacekeeper, evil empire, and targeting doctrine make us suspicious. What are these words hiding, we ask; and who is killed when a nuclear event happens?

If language cannot make oppressed groups disappear, it is often used to demean and insult them. Women become "girls," spouses are "little women," feminists are "castrating bitches," women religious are "the good Sisters." Such language, often openly hostile, becomes itself a weapon. It makes it possible to dismiss those we don't accept, and to ignore what they represent. Often when I have spoken with groups about nuclear questions, a man has questioned the facts I present or the viewpoint I propose. In these instances I have almost always been addressed as "honey," or "dear."

One does not take "honey" seriously, nor does one pay attention to what she says. This pattern is repeated again and again each day in every facet of life. It has caused some women to learn how to shout; it has made most women angry. It has also taught us a lesson: language as weapon is invalid language. Language which demeans or dismisses anyone is false. That lesson has significant ramifications for war and peace. Victims themselves, women are *very* slow to accept the dismissal of others as naive, communists, leftists, demagogues, hysterical, or evil. The propaganda doesn't work, because we know — from experience — *how* it works. Wounded ourselves, women tend to identify more readily with those at whom the weapons are aimed than with those who aim them. Questioning sexist language inevitably involves questioning nuclear language.

Language can also exclude people. Anyone who has ever travelled to a foreign country knows this. There are many foreign countries for women. Technical terms or in-house jargon have kept many from being full partners in the discussion. How many women, one wonders, have submitted to unnecessary surgical procedures because they didn't understand their doctor's language and were too intimidated to tell him? How many others have lost a promotion because they didn't "speak our language"? Roman Catholic seminaries were closed to women for centuries. One justification for this was language. All seminary courses were taught in Latin; women didn't know Latin. But the foremost place to learn Latin was in the seminary itself, and women couldn't study at the seminary.

Patterns of speaking can also exclude supposed partners in dialogue. Although women are generally perceived as "great talkers," it is really men who do most of the talking. Susan Brownmiller refers to this in her book, *Femininity*.[5] "In one systematic analysis of taped conversations between men and women," she says, "the men did 98% of the interrupting."

There are many reasons why men interrupt the speech of women and get away with it. For one thing, more men have been trained to be verbally aggressive. In law school an argumentative, disputatious style is practiced in the classroom to sharpen combative skills. Courses for salesmen include training in how to make an effective stand-up presentation and how to be persuasive. But more to the point, boys grow up assuming they have valuable information to impart. By tradition girls were instructed by their mothers and advised by their teen magazines that the most appreciated quality in a young lady is her ability to listen, to play dumb on dates and to act impressed in male company.[6]

Made invisible, dismissed and excluded, many women have not only protested against sexist language, they have also begun to seriously question its very premises. Inclusive language has come to mean much more than merely taking account of sex differences. Previously when women were uncomfortable with abstract language and dualistic categories, they felt something was wrong with them. They had, of course, been conditioned to feel that way. Now many ask, rather, if there isn't something wrong with the language.

This questioning has in turn led to a suspicion of the prevailing language and even to a "hermeneutics of suspicion."[7] This method of interpretation, which originated in the theological disciplines, is significant for all reception of language. Recognizing that the language system is structured by the dominant group within a culture, a hermeneutics of suspicion tests that language against the lived experience of other, non-dominant groups. Words and expressions are no longer accepted at face value; the bias from which they come is critically examined and any inaccuracies are pointed out. Such interpretation includes acknowledgement of the writer/ speaker's world view in its understanding of language.

Critical interpretation has massive ramifications in understanding history, ecclesiastical traditions and sacred texts.[8] It is also vitally important for nuclear language; it dares to say that the patriarchal, hierarchical, abstract vocabulary of the nuclear age is in fact upside down, disfigured language. When the Pentagon says that more nuclear bombs are necessary to protect our national security, many people recognize that they do not feel more secure because there are more weapons in the world. They question what "security" means for the speakers and, most importantly, they speak out and offer alternative definitions of this rare and precious commodity.

Suspicion also characterizes how one hears the myriad of euphemisms abroad in the land. What (who!) is behind collateral damages, counter value targeting, launch-on warnings? What do these mean in terms of persons, of lives saved or lost, of worlds destroyed or preserved? Many of us have asked these questions before, but we often did so convinced that we just couldn't understand. Now we recognize that we understand only too well, and more and more we refuse to stand under such lan-

guage. When questions are unashamedly posed, sad truths
sometimes emerge.

When the Bishops' committee met with the Arms Control
and Disarmament Agency, I experienced one of the most personally saddening moments of the many months and many meetings of the committee's work. At the end of a somewhat unpleas-
ant time with members of the Agency, I was escorted to the entrance of the State Department building by a very pleasant
young man who had been present. He apologized that some
members of the Agency had talked too much and regretted the
fact that we hadn't been able to hear more about new advances
in targeting.

He then enthusiastically descibed these advances for me.
Nuclear weapons were becoming so accurate that they could hit
a single building within a complex of buildings, he said. "But
how many people do they kill?" I asked. Startled, he again
explained to me (of course, he presumed I had not understood)
how pin-point targeting could destroy one building and not have
to destroy a whole military installation, or a neighborhood. This
was a wonderful advance! I replied, "But it still kills people,
doesn't it?" He was quiet for a moment, and then said, "Yes.
That's why I got out of it [that area of defense planning]." And
yet he was telling me about it with the fervor of an evangelist.
What happens to people, I wondered, as I left that huge building. What happens that makes them so convinced about something they know is so deadly? Perhaps it is the living of a double
life, made possible to a great extent by language that hides
deadly truth. Perhaps it is too many unasked questions.

Feminist studies have provided us with valuable insights
into the power of language to obscure, distort, destroy. They
have given us valuable tools for the recognition and interpretation of such language and have challenged all of us to use these
tools. They have also begun to transform the language itself.
Recognizing the inability of patriarchal language to fully express feminine experience, women writers, poets, and musi-

cians have started speaking in their own voices, and in so doing have offered us new visions, new perspectives, new hope for a world transformed. Sometimes feminist language, in its struggle to articulate the feminine experience, astonishes and may even perplex us. Mary Daly's writings are one such example. Seeking to retrieve and recover language from its patriarchal distortions, she uses old words in new ways and previously negative images become positive ones. Spinsters and hags and witches are favorable images for her. Common words are used in uncommon ways. Daly talks about "positive paranoia," "the State of Positively Revolting Hags," and about "Spinster-Spooking," which is "re-calling/re-membering/re-claiming our Witches' power to cast spells, to charm, to overcome prestige with prestidigitation, to cast glamours, to employ occult grammar, to enthrall, to bewitch."[9]

Other women coin new words. Radically different from nuclear language, these words stress caring and relationship and emotion. Alice Walker's "womanist," for example, indicates a woman who, among other things, "Loves music. Loves dance. Loves the moon. *Loves* the Spirit. Loves love and food and roundness. Loves struggle. *Loves* the folk. Loves herself. *Regardless.*"[10] Still others tell new stories or retell ancient tales in feminine ways, as do Rosemary Ruether in "The Kenosis of the Father: A Feminist Midrash on the Gospel in Three Acts,"[11] and Judith Plaskow in her account of creation in "The Coming of Lilith."[12] Many insist on new forms of writing, as does Robin Morgan.

> This book attempts . . . to view feminism in its three- and even four-dimensional character, as the holograph I believe it is. That has required that the form of writing itself attempt to project, reflect, and express the content — to move beyond a rigid, linear, single-genre approach toward a contrapuntal style which risks blending a personal voice with analytical and philosophical ones, interweaving parables,

dramatic format, and meditative structure with journalistic reportage and theoretical hypotheses.[13]

To read feminist literature is to enter a new world for some. For many women, however, it is their own world, their own experiences, suspicions, and instinctive knowings which they encounter. "Womanist" language is filled with life, it is about people and caring, connections and mutuality. It is inclusive language that reveals rather than hides, empowers instead of demeans, participates but doesn't dominate. "The language of a people is its fate," says Wilder. When women's language enters into the public sphere, particularly the nuclear sphere, the fate of our people brightens perceptively. One has only to imagine, for instance, a military budget written by a feminist or a womanist.

Logic

One of the most important functions of feminist language is the challenge it poses to the absolute supremacy of abstract logic. "It's not that we don't *understand* it," women say, "it's that we don't *believe* it." Barbara Starrett describes such logic as:

A way of thinking that can be described as objective, Aristotelian, data-centered, descriptive, measuring, hierarchical, systematic, fragmentizing, logical, sequential. It is also anti-emotional, cold, impersonal, unfeeling, sterile and passive. It has carefully defined rules and limits; within those limits there is consistency and predictability. Outside the limits is fear and madness.[14]

Women have, of course, functioned within this mode of thinking. They have had to. It was considered the only acceptable, serious way of thinking. If one wished to have the proper "credentials," she had to be able to function well in the system.

Most women, however, have always felt a sense of dis-ease within such modes of thought, have felt a subtle yet consistent discomfort which made them doubt their own abilities. The worship of abstract, rational thought has so deeply permeated our culture that other ways of thinking, of viewing reality, are perceived as inferior and as "feminine." Woman's intuition, for example, might help in detecting an unfaithful husband or the change in a child's cry, but it had no significance in the "real" world.

As women have had to learn to function in this "real" world and to employ its way of thinking, so too have they been victims of it. They (and all oppressed peoples) have been defined by its theories, their bodies have been regulated by its scientific studies, their psyches interpreted according to its psychological theories, their morality evaluated by its standards. The raising of women's consciousness has enabled women to say that this is wrong, that their experience of life, of law, of their own bodies and souls was different from that descibed for them by the male system. Perhaps the most crucial aspect of any movement toward liberation is that of reflection on one's own experience. When a person becomes conscious of what happens in her life, of the meaning of these happenings, of patterns which appear and reappear, one recognizes oneself as a person — a valuable person. She begins to love herself, *regardless*.

Since such reflection always takes place in relation to others, the individual recognizes that her experience is not without parallel in others' lives. This affirms, empowers, and challenges her. "If so many of us have felt this discomfort, have not fit the definitions, function only with trepidation, perhaps it's not me, not even us. Perhaps it's the system itself which is inadequate." And so begins the transformation — or the revolution! Old, ancient, undervalued ways of thinking are retrieved and honored, a new consciousness appears. Starrett describes this phenomenon:

But a new and radical consciousness is emerging, primarily through women, and despite our massive conditioning. Women have been 'allowed,' in our exclusion from important roles in the male structures, to develop other ways of knowing, thinking and being. These ways can be described as emotional, direct, expressive, intuitive, immediate, subjective, relationship-centered.[15]

· What is important here is not so much that women think differently — they have done so for centuries — but that they (and many men) say that such differences are valid and necessary. They dare to insist that these ways belong in the public sphere, in academia, in government, diplomacy, and science. This development is of crucial significance for war and peace, and terror. Its significance lies mainly in the fact that elements of the human experience which are foundational to the creation of a peaceful world, stand a chance of being owned, acknowledged, and influential.

Feminine logic has long seemed a contradiction in terms to many; it is rather an expansion in terms. Feminine logic does not deny the importance of clear, rational, objective thought, nor does it dismiss scientific theories and hypotheses. It values these, but does not idolize them. Other factors, other types of knowledge must be taken into account if one is to come to truth, say feminist thinkers, and facts must always be placed within their human context if they are to have any meaning. Such ways of thinking have specific characteristics which are present in all areas of research: from the academic to the literary to the historical to the everyday ponderings of women seeking to understand their lives.

Primary to feminine logic is the presence of persons. Abstract thought is always related in some way to human beings, either in terms of how the facts will affect persons ("How many people are killed by the new targeting strategies?"); or in terms of the persons who formulated the "truth" ("How can we know the real truth about witches if their stories are only told by witch hunters?"); or, finally, of the persons who are themselves the articulators of facts ("How does this interpretation relate to my own experience?"). The importance of persons and of relationships influences the way decisions are made, particularly in terms of moral judgments.

In her study of feminine moral development,[16] Carol Gilligan relates the example of a young boy named Jake and a young girl named Amy. Both were asked to resolve a moral dilemma. A poor man, Heinz, had a very sick wife who needed an expensive medicine in order to be healed. Heinz, however, could not afford the medicine. Should he steal it? Jake answered in the affirmative — in terms of logic. "For one thing, a human life is worth more than money, and if the druggist only makes $1,000, he is still going to live, but if Heinz doesn't steal the drug, his wife is going to die."[17] Amy, on the other hand, had a more difficult time making a decision. She did not feel that Heinz should steal the drug, but rather that he should talk to the druggist and make him more aware of his wife's need for the medicine. Gilligan points out that what is happening here is that two different ways of viewing moral judgment are at work. Jake views the dilemma as " 'sort of like a math problem with humans,' he sets it up as an equation and proceeds to work out the solution."[18] Amy views the same dilemma in terms of the persons involved and their ongoing relationships. The "logic of the justice approach" confronts an "ethic of care."[19]

Like so many women, Amy finds it extremely difficult to make a judgment based on facts or logic alone. Traditionally, this tendency has been viewed as an inadequacy and as reason why women should not be in decision-making roles in the public sphere. Rather than inadequate, however, this 'feminine' trait is of great advantage in situations where the lives of human beings are at stake. Whereas feminine logic is reluctant to sacrifice life for an abstract principle, it is often willing to sacrifice for

another person. The woman who rescued the heroine of Isabel
Allende's story is such a woman. She risked her life not for some
principle, but for another woman who was in need of her. The
Mothers of the Plaza faced danger each time they appeared in
public. They did so not because they sought to defend abstract
"justice," but because their loved ones had disappeared. When
feminine logic looks to war, it does not view it in terms of
strategic advantages or battles won or national security. It sees
men and women and children who may die.

Olive Schreiner spoke with such logic when she wrote:

> There is, perhaps, no woman . . . who could look
> down upon a battlefield covered with slain, but the
> thought would rise in her, 'So many mothers' sons
> . . . So many months of weariness and pain while
> bones and muscles were shaped within; so many
> hours of anguish and struggle that breath might be;
> so many baby mouths drawing life at woman's
> breasts; all this, that men might lie with glazed
> eyeballs, and swollen bodies, and fixed, blue, un-
> closed mouths, and great limbs tossed — this, that an
> acre of ground might be manured with human flesh.
> . . .' No woman who is a woman says of a human
> body, 'It is nothing!'
>
> On that day, when the woman takes her place be-
> side the man in the governance and arrangement of
> external affairs of her race will also be that day that
> heralds the death of war as a means of arranging
> human differences.[20]

The thought patterns characteristically viewed as
'feminine' would be most discomfiting in laboratories where nuclear weapons are viewed as interesting problems. They would
be equally out of place in discussions of the amount of dirt, the
need for x-number of shovels, the availability of doors for shel-

ters. This discomfort is not a sign that such thought patterns don't belong in such discussions, rather it is sure indication that something is lacking in both the discussions and in the laboratories.

Whereas masculine logic is marked by objectivity and impartiality, feminine logic is subjective and decidedly partial. It is subjective in that it takes the person with all of her experiences into account. A scripture scholar, for example, can no longer study a text only in terms of its vocabulary, structure, and variants. She must now ask what the text says to/of her as a woman. And, knowing that the text was worded by men, she must question it. When studying nuclear questions and nuclear theories, she cannot not ask what they mean in terms of her own life and the lives of those whom she loves. Often such questions are seen as "muddying the waters." They seem to come out of nowhere and to have no relation to the matter at hand. On the contrary, they *are* the matter at hand. Justice, freedom, defense of our country, national security — these mean nothing to the dead.

Women have recognized that to know abstract, theoretical knowledge is not enough. They have begun to ask how that knowledge is used. Does it continue patterns of oppression and degradation? Will it lead to the annihilation of our world? Logic and truth are not simply 'there;' they do something, they influence our lives. Feminine logic takes this into account and seeks — actively — to affect the way our lives are either manipulated or liberated by such logic and 'truth'. Facts, then, are not viewed as absolutes, their ambiguity is also considered. Truth becomes more of a living reality which slowly, tortuously unfolds among us. Judgments are more difficult to make, as they were for Amy, because the texture of the dilemma is no longer two-dimensional, and everyone is affected by the outcome. The purity of concepts is colored, enhanced, perhaps diminished by the participation of the knower. History for women becomes the history of the oppressed, the unwritten stories, the *her*story. And war is viewed from the victims' eyes.

Feminine logic, then, expands the meaning of logic in that it involves persons and the human context in its knowing, it owns its own subjectivity, and it considers participation an integral aspect. It also honors such illogical faculties as imagination, vision, and emotions. Lifton maintains that the key to the world's survival lies in awareness. Awareness, he says, "involves the full work and play of the imagination. It means imagining the danger that is real, but also imagining possibilities beyond that danger, forms of thought and action beyond immediate assumptions."[21] One of the most troubling aspects of U.S. diplomacy in recent years is its woeful lack of imagination. There seem to be very few ways to deal with conflict. In fact, force and military tactics seem to be the only way of resolving differences. Social, political, ethical problems are all treated as military problems, and military solutions are the only ones offered. Imagination would call for examining — even creating — other ways to resolve differences and to deal with conflict.

Imagination, a gift consistently called forth in women's scholarship, celebration, and contemplation, invites one to envision other possibilites than the *status quo*. It enables us to look at what could happen in our world — the potential tragedy as well as the hoped-for future. When I have spoken with groups about the nuclear terror, I have consistently been struck by our inability to imagine a world after nuclear war. This is partly due to a necessary psychic numbing. The horror is too great to contemplate. It is also due, however, to our inability to think creatively, to envision that which is not in the textbooks.

This same inability is even more obvious when it comes to imagining a peaceful world. Many of us are simply incapable of such wild dreams. And yet, if we cannot imagine it, how can we begin to create it? One of the most significant activities of peace groups, I am convinced, is that of encouraging children to write about, to draw, to paint a peaceful world. Perhaps the most wonderful and most ignored peace activity in recent years was the creation of the Peace Ribbon which was wrapped around the

Pentagon on August 4, 1985. The vision of Justine Merritt became the creative activity of hundreds of thousands of men, women, and children. Asked to make a banner showing what people could not "bear to think of as lost forever in a nuclear war," people all over the world responded with creations of beauty, hope, and marvelous imagination. The title of this chapter is taken from one of the thousands of banners made by persons seeking peace with their hands, their gifts, and their imaginations.[22] It is within that most creative of our human capacities, imagination, that the possibility for a transformed society rests. In this sense, it is the most "logical" of all thought.

Oppressed persons have always been more sensitive to imagination. It offers a hope of freedom in a killing world. This imagination has allowed them (and us) to dream dreams and paint visions of another world. These dreams and visions have sustained thousands upon thousands throughout history. Too often, however, they have been viewed as "daydreams," escapes from reality which served to perpetuate oppression. But visions are profoundly powerful, they exert a strong and pervasive influence on the present. If the vision is strong enough, it conditions the way we live in the here and now. We begin to live toward that vision. Recent studies in futurology have stressed the importance of designing (imagining, really) the desired future. Once a group can own that future, they can find ways to begin to create it.

Change is never achieved when thought is limited to rational logic, nor is transformation possible if the discourse remains that of denunciation of the evils of the present. Alternatives are necessary, and alternatives most often present themselves to our imagination and in our visions. The women's movement is intensely conscious of this. Recognition of the oppression in women's history as well as in the life of every woman was only the beginning. Other possibilities, other ways of living together in our world slowly emerged in discussions, papers, statements, legislative initiatives. Visions made themselves known, strategies for realizing them were discovered. When this began to happen, struggle inevitably intensified, for not all people shared the same vision, not all agreed with the chosen strategies, most were unsure of the new terrain in which they found themselves. The power of the vision, worded in myriad ways, has continued to sustain, however, and has engendered alternative modes of being and of relating in the very midst of the struggle.

The healing of nuclear terror demands conversion; it requires the courage to look at ourselves as we are: terrorized yet numb, bemoaning our fate yet seemingly unable to change it, rational yet mad. Conversion also demands that our mirror offer us a glimpse of who we could be. Imagination and vision provide that glimpse. They offer us a hope in the future and in ourselves which no set of facts can provide. Without them we remain at best unchanged, at worst lost in the despair of being unable to change even though we know we are doomed. The expansion of "respectable" thought to include these two invaluable elements which has taken place so profoundly in the women's movement has offered the world a way to peace in the only places peace can begin: the heart, the mind, the dream. Feminism has also claimed respectability for another reality which has long been anathema to rationalistic thought: emotions.

As we have seen in Chapter Three, public and private display of emotions are taken as a sure sign of weakness, intellectual inferiority, and/or demagoguery in the male-dominated world. Jean Baker Miller writes:

> In our dominant tradition, however, it [emotionality] has not been seen as an aid to understanding and action, but rather as an impediment, even an evil. We have a long tradition of trying to dispense with, or at least to control or neutralize, emotionality, rather than valuing, embracing, and cultivating its contributing strengths.[23]

Emotions are suspect. They are also connected with women. Women are emotional; therefore, women are weak, suspect. No human being is without emotions, but because they are signs of weakness, they are threatening to the "strong" within a society. Therefore, they are declared the domain of the inferiors. Women have long been the carriers of emotion for society and as such have preserved a vital aspect of humanity even as they have been perceived as inferior for so doing. The acknowledgment and expression of emotion, so decried in the nuclear arena ("if you allow the emotion of nuclear war to enter the Defense Department, you'd end up totally paralyzed"), is one of the absolutely basic keys to the healing of nuclear terror.

"A generation which does not get angry about its future is a generation preparing to die." When Congressman Ron Dellums made this statement at a seminar which I attended, he spoke to the heart of my discomfort at the extremely "cool heads" which appeared at the conference table of many of the meetings of the Bishops' committee. Although it was "unseemly" to get angry, to express fear when speaking with administration officials, I knew I experienced those emotions — painfully — and I could not help but wonder if I was caught in nuclear madness, or if others were. Anger often springs from love disregarded or thwarted. Love of ourselves ("regardless"), for another, for our earth is made angry when it contemplates destruction. To deny that anger and to repress the energy generated by such strong feeling is to block an incredible source of power for change.

Anger is perhaps the most complex of the many emotions related to nuclear terror. I think this is because it appears in so many guises. In the first place, the anger which springs from sorrow at the loss of what is so precious to us often appears as rage at the persons who serve to "make clear the path" not to salvation, but to destruction. Pentagon officials become easy targets even though violence against individuals is war in microcosm. It often becomes very difficult to differentiate between the person who speaks for the system and the system itself. It is hard, in anger, to remember that the transformation of peacemaking involves global changes and demands that such systemic changes be made in non-violent ways. The line between protesting the unjust, violent system and the words and actions which perpetuate that system, and the human beings who speak those words, perform those actions, and are themselves part of the system, is very faint and difficult to see even at the best of times. Anger also arises from thwarted domination. Thus, challengers of the *status quo* often find themselves the objects of anger; they are demeaned, punished, made to question themselves.

Most significantly, I think, anger is an acceptable male emotion. Most of our society regards anger in men as a sign of manliness and virility. The soldier is taught to use rage in battle, the football player is urged to "Go out there and get those. . . ." This particular emotion, then, belongs to men. When women are openly and vocally angry, they are viewed as out of control, hysterical, or (worse) "masculine." The anger of women often enrages men. Women have stepped out of the stereotype, they have invaded the male prerogative.

Helen Caldicott gives a chilling example of this in *Missile Envy*.[24] She appeared on a talk show with a retired General who remained calm and rational throughout the interview. After the show had finished, the General came to her and told her that she should go to Russia. She responded in an anger which sprang from fear. "I fucking want my kids to grow up," she said. The General became so enraged by her response — an angry one, and one which used language unacceptable for a "lady" — that he tried to physically attack her. The studio technicians had to restrain him. The scene is chilling because it uncovers the thinly veiled rage present in nuclear discussions and because it suggests in blatant form the response which openly emotional challengers can expect to receive. Lifton says that one of the valuable effects of imagining the real and new future is that one ceases to be a victim. To withstand the rage of the powerful, to continue to speak and to act are actions which demand that we cease being victims. Women, who know only too well the danger of showing anger toward those who dominate them, are learning to withstand and to continue. This speaks of pain for everyone; it speaks of hope for peace.

Anger is not the only emotion involved in nuclear terror, however. There are others for which anger often stands as symptom. Among these are fear, despair, and sorrow. It is obvious that anyone who pays attention to the nuclear threat experiences a fear which rapidly escalates into a terror which threatens to paralyze. When that terror is combined with a sense of powerlessness, it produces despair. Surrounded by despair, we tend to resort to the strategies outlined by Lifton: denial, numbing, double lives. We are encouraged to do so because fear is viewed as weakness. It is "unmanly" to be afraid and to own that fear. Yet it is only in facing fear that we learn its source and its remedy. Joanna Rogers Macy[25] speaks to the necessity of owning our fears if we would transform our despair. To speak aloud of terror and to know that others share the same feelings is to begin to search for ways of healing. Healing of the paralysis of despair starts when we expose it to the light and especially when we touch other persons in the midst of it. To know we are not alone is to reach into another's strength and to find our own.

Information itself is never enough. We need to recognize our responses to that information, and we need to be conscious that others have those same responses. Nuclear terror is not a sign of weakness or of neurosis; on the contrary, it is a sure sign of health and of sanity. Women have always been "allowed" to own their fears; they have in fact been encouraged to do so, for their fears enhanced the strength of their men. I believe that women have always known that their fears were not the result of some weakness but rather the product of their honest and correct evaluations of a situation. It is vitally important that women continue to speak of fear and that they own it as strength, not weakness. In so doing, emotion itself is redeemed and allowed to function as the teacher it is.

There are moments when the world is too beautiful to bear. A blazing, purple-red-gold-blue sunset upon an undisturbed snow; pheasants wobbling (but pretending they are strutting) across that snow together; the silence of a Grecian hilltop broken only by the sound of a shepherd and the sheep: each of us knows her/his own moments. They stop us, fill us with silence, render us inadequate before the wonder. Sometimes they fill us with sorrow. There are moments, too, when human beings are too beautiful to bear: little children crossing a street on their way home from school; an aging parent still intensely conscious of any sign of pain in her children even when she notices little else; a quiet, timid friend choosing life and finding new, amazing courage. Each of us has known the awe such encounters produce.

And each of us knows that in this awe we are sometimes surprised by sorrow. There are myriad reasons/meanings for sorrow, but an overwhelming one is the sense that all of this and all of these are in danger of annihilation. To grieve the loss of our beautiful earth, of amazing human beings is to recognize our love for them and our connectedness with all of life. Such grief is holy for it touches the deepest heart of us even as it reaches beyond us into life itself. Yet public expressions of this grief are perceived as weakness and demagoguery. As with fear, grieving openly is a womanly thing; it is for men to keep the stiff upper lip. Public grief at the spectre of the destruction of the earth is not to be taken seriously. Such grief is very real, however, and very serious. It is a powerful and profound expression of what the existence of nuclear weapons and the threat of their use have done to us. It is also a genuine, meaningful reflection of what they *could* do to all of us and to our world. Grief that is strong and unabashed releases the grip of "reason" which threatens to paralyze our courage. It frees us to act, as the Mothers of the Plaza have so eloquently shown us. It is for women to claim that which they have been allowed, to name it as human and holy, and to allow — demand, if necessary — that such grief be heeded.

Feminist "logic," far from being inferior to the objective, abstract, emotionless thought systems of the male-dominated culture, is broader, wider, and deeper. It does not allow for the separation of the mind from the person, nor the separation of the person from the human reality. It claims value for all that is human — our imagination, our ability to feel, our capacity to wonder and to grieve — and insists that these dimensions are necessary in both private and public decision-making. "Limited" nuclear war is never sane when it is seen in terms of persons, of imagining its effects, of rage at annihilation, of owned, real fear, of human, holy grief. Peace becomes possible when persons reach out to each other in all of their reality, especially their "weakness." It is persons who make peace, not abstract theories. But it may well be reliance on "strength" and on "interesting physics problems" which will destroy us. When we ask which will prevail, we come again to the question of power.

Power

As logic has been transformed, so too has power. While some women sought greater equality through entrance into the male power structure and learned very well how to function within that system, power remained a very negative concept for most women. It represented the oppressive manipulation that so many had experienced. There was a rejection of that which had injured so many. As women found their voices, however, accepted understandings of power were questioned. Rather than reject power *per se,* many began to redefine it and to rediscover the true meaning of power as energy and movement. Power as energy, as the ability to be what you are, as an open system, as power-with or power-to, has become very important to women and to the possibility of a transformed world. Marilyn French, in her painstaking work *Beyond Power,*[26] maintains that the central value of Western society is power expressed as control and domination. Power, she says, is man's way to attain transcendence over that which might control him: the body, the

earth, nature. She shows how self-defeating such attempts are
and calls for the development of "power-to," available to all
peoples and expressed in nurturance, caring, and delight. She is
one of many writers and scholars whose theories (which come
out of experience as well as books) provide new, more peaceable
kinds of power.

Starting from the fundamental understanding of power as
energy and movement, many women claim power as unlimited
energy released when persons share in relationships. Joanna
Rogers Macy writes of the power-with that functions "from the
bottom up" in an open system. It is not "a property one can own,"
but rather a "process one opens to."[27] It thrives in interaction
and is open to feedback and to change. This kind of power is not
a commodity available to the few, prized-above-all possessions,
guarded most jealously, "more addictive than any drug, more
seductive than sex;" it is something which happens, an energy
released in human interraction. Rather than destructive, *this*
power is creative and life-enhancing. It is open to imagination
and to caring. It is also open to everyone. It is, therefore, non-
hierarchical and non-controlling. If I do not need to protect my
power, I do not need to dominate another. If I find my personal
power enhanced by another's ability to be what she/he can be
and do what she/he can do, then I encourage the other's participation and value collaboration more than control.

Women's groups are often portrayed as somewhat "fuzzy"
in their functioning. They never seem to get anything done.
They sit around and talk all the time without any direction.
They don't have any products; they keep asking how everyone
"feels" about anything and everything. What these groups are
doing is discovering ways of power. Rather than top-down control, they are functioning in an ever-widening collaboration.
This is not fuzziness but rather conscious, disciplined efforts to
be inclusive of all who are part of the group, to tap into every
person's wisdom, to enable every person to contribute to the en-
richment of all. The "product" of such groups is to be seen in the

process itself. Marked by a hard-won mutuality (for women, too, have been trained in hierarchical power), these organizations/ meetings/gatherings result in the empowerment of untold numbers of formerly powerless individuals.

Such an understanding of power is often viewed as ridiculous within a hierarchical world. It is declared weak and ineffective. Nothing important can be accomplished by those who can't "take control." It is sometimes seen as dangerous. Painful confrontations often occur when the two views come into conflict. Such is the case in the recent and ongoing problems concerning the official, hierarchical sanction of the Constitutions of U.S. women's religious congregations. The section of these various Constitutions which is almost always considered unacceptable is that dealing with governance and authority. Many women's communities have become convinced of the value of shared authority and of power exercised in mutuality. When they try to express this in describing their modes of governance in community, those who function in and believe in hierarchical, controlling power find it unacceptable and the Constitutions are not approved.

The response of most of these communities gives further evidence of different understandings of power. The community decides together on its response to the Vatican critiques. They engage in processes which appear to many to be inefficient, but which are essential to the women whose experience is expressed in their Constitutions. Long, prayerful discussions ensue among all of the members. Statements are viewed in the light of the Gospel and in terms of their accuracy in describing both the already of experience and the not-yet of ideals. In many cases, this process leads to an affirmation by the women religious that what they have written is true to them and to their mission. Such an affirmation can sometimes result in the perception by the hierarchy that the particular community is "disobedient" or unfaithful to the intent of their foundresses/founders. Disobedience and infidelity are not at stake in these conflicts. What really happens is a confrontation between two differing visions of power.

Patriarchal power functions in secrecy, rigidity, and "from strength." Feminist power chooses openness, fluidity and vulnerability. One of the commonplace "truths" about women is their innate inability to keep secrets. This stereotype is omnipresent. It even reaches into the minutiae of academic research. One of the unsolved questions in New Testament research, for example, is that of the true authorship of the *Epistle to the Hebrews*. The highly respected scholar Adolf Harnack proposed Priscilla as the author. One of his reasons: the true authorship has always been unknown, as it would have been if a woman wrote it. His theory never met with much acceptance, however. One of the reasons against it: women cannot keep secrets. If a woman had really written *Hebrews*, everyone would have known it!

Undoubtedly, this stereotype has been perpetuated because it justified the keeping of secrets from women. If "knowledge is power," sharing knowledge implies sharing power, something unacceptable in a patriarchal atmosphere. A vision of power as open-ended and collaborative has no need to "protect" knowledge. On the contrary, it thrives in discussion and interaction. Secrecy is not as important as energy. Further, secrecy has become an anathema for many women because it has been used against them. Demands for secrecy have kept women from finding support when they most needed it, have deprived them of their rights in courts of law and in ecclesiastical conflicts, have threatened their lives and the lives of all who walk the earth. Women, as victims of men's secrets, value reverence in personal confidentiality, but they do not value the hidden machinations of a power elite — in the church, the boardroom, the Cabinet offices.

In feminist power, rigidity is replaced with fluidity. The images of human interaction are not linear ones or those of ladders which must be climbed. They are, rather, circular ones; circles can always grow, can always be stretched to include more persons. Ladders don't expand to include more climbers, they just keep getting higher. Such fluidity influences one's view of dissent and of conflict. Whereas a different opinion or a challenging question is viewed as threat in a rigid power system, in an open one opinions and questions are rightly seen as opportunities for growth.

Jean C. Lambert has written an article which shows the latter position as it functions in feminist biblical scholarship. In "An F Factor? The New Testament in Some White Feminist Christian Theological Construction,"[28] Lambert analyzes the similarities and differences among four women scholars. One similarity which she finds in the midst of many differences is the "F Factor." She describes it as

> . . . a critical, patient, stubborn generosity toward divergent opinions. In more metaphoric terms, one might envision it as a willingness to journey with a mixed multitude because the company is challenging and freeing, and to entertain the possibility that destinations initially understood as different may turn out to be on the same continent after all.[29]

Lambert comments on the source of this stubborn generosity.

> I believe this generosity has to do more properly with a tough-mindedness some women are learning as we come to terms with our own oppression and note the ways we turn oppression against ourselves and our sisters. "Generosity" pertains to a discipline of 'sisterhood' that refuses to deny the truth one sees even though it involves criticizing a sister, and yet refuses to treat the sister as less than a valuable contributor to the discussion.[30]

It is fascinating to imagine an "F Factor" at work in the Pentagon or at the negotiating tables!

Differences of opinions, dissenting voices, then, are not regarded with horror. They are not stifled, rather they are met with wonderful, "stubborn generosity." Within this context the meaning of conflict is also transformed.

> All of us, but women especially, are taught to see conflict as something frightening and evil. These connotations have been assigned by the dominant group and have obscured the necessity for conflict. Even more crucially, they obscure the fundamental nature of reality — the fact that, in its most basic sense, conflict is inevitable, the source of all growth, and an absolute necessity if one is to be alive.[31]

Jean Baker Miller sums up both the "old" view of conflict (frightening, evil), and the "new" (inevitable, source of growth, a necessity) in these sentences. No one is a stranger to conflict, especially no woman whose consciousness has been raised in these past twenty years. We have met it in every facet of our personal and political lives. And we have all been accused of creating it. Baker Miller points out that whenever any subordinate group steps outside the stereotypes created for it by the dominant group, open conflict inevitably results. She goes on to say, however, that the conflict is not created by this action. It was already there. "That is, women are not *creating* conflict; they are exposing the fact that conflict exists."[32] Instead of being villains (witches?), women are contributing to the growth of all of society by exposing the hidden (and therefore insidious) conflicts which have long been operative among us. In so doing, they have enabled many of us to lose our fear of conflict and to learn how to live with it and to live humanely within it. This demands discipline, courage, and a constant, insistent call to conversion. Conflict is not resolved by force but by mutual understanding, despite what our male leaders tell us. Such an understanding of conflict is vitally important within the sphere of the multiple "world conflicts" of today. Tragically, it is not there.

Another aspect of rigid power is its lack of capacity for self-examination. It is nearly impossible for those who dominate to question their motives. They are too busy questioning the motives of others. The women's movement always begins in the raising of consciousness; it always continues in reflection upon women's experience. Both of these processes demand self-examination and self-questioning. Further, the women's movement has demanded that women challenge the definitions of who they are which have been given to them by men. This has been an extremely painful thing for most women to do, because they have been trained to look to men for meaning and approbation. The good opinion of father or Father, of the boss (almost always male), of the boyfriend or potential husband, has always carried tremendous significance for most women. To forego that in the name of truth and freedom is a costly venture, one which simply cannot be achieved without long and arduous self-examination. Honest self-knowledge frees us in that it eliminates much of our need to pretend that we are perfect human beings. It also makes us more understanding of other persons who are not themselves perfect. I believe that it makes us more peaceable, for we do not need to defend ourselves or our power against any who would challenge the image. As long as power is unreflective it remains domination and is thus extremely liable to corruption.

Power-with, open as it is, requires vulnerability. Rather than fearing the possibility of becoming vulnerable as men do, women simply are vulnerable. Their physical strength is generally less than that of men, and their economic security is most often dependent upon men. Vulnerability is not a dreaded spectre to them, it is a constant reality. Threats of a "window of vulnerability" mean little to women who live in a world of vulnerability. And from within that world, women have offered a different perspective. Positive vulnerability implies openness to

others and to one's own emotions. It enables persons to come together in sensitivity and in caring and to find amazing strength
in the reality of shared pain. Isabel Allende's woman rescuer is
a very vulnerable person; perhaps that is why she is so coura-
geous in the face of another's suffering. The problem is not that
"we" might become vulnerable, but that there is so little mutual
vulnerability in our culture. If there were more, there would undoubtedly be fewer breakdowns among those who cannot ask for
comfort because John Wayne never asked for a hug. There
would also be less violence.

A fluid, open power does not need to resort to force to protect
itself. It does not find it necessary to be the strongest in order to
validate itself. Power which functions best in collaboration
needs to be a gentle, reverential power. It does not batter those
who disagree but rather welcomes them. Women and children
are the primary victims of violence in our culture. They are
acutely conscious of its horror and its futility. Feminist power
eschews violence even as it continues to name it in all of its manifestations. In doing so, women actively seek to undermine a
fundamental prop of patriarchal power and thus open the way
to profound transformation.

Relationship

Throughout our discussion of feminine language, logic, and
power, women's proclivity to view everything — from pronouns
to theory to coercion — in terms of persons and relationships has
been obvious. There is good reason for this. Recent studies have
made clear what most women always felt but never really understood: the very growth and development of women takes
place in terms of and within the context of relationships. Both
Jean Baker Miller and Carol Gilligan emphasize the centrality
of relationship in the growth of women. Baker Miller writes
that, "One central feature [of women's development] is that
women stay with, build on, and develop in a context of attach-

ment and affiliation with others. Indeed, women's sense of self becomes very much organized around being able to make and then to maintain affiliations and relationships."[33] Gilligan states, "Thus in all of the women's descriptions, identity is defined in a context of relationship and judged by a standard of responsibility and care."[34] They both contrast this mode of growth with the until now "accepted" growth pattern of individuation and achievement. Baker Miller describes the contrast:

> We all begin life deeply attached to the people around us. Men, or boys, are encouraged to move out of this state of existence — in which they and their fate are intimately intertwined in the lives and fate of other people. Women are encouraged to remain in this state but, as they grow, to transfer their attachment to a male figure.
>
> Boys are rewarded for developing other aspects of themselves. These other factors — power or skills — gradually begin to displace some of the importance of affiliations and eventually to supersede them. There is no question that women develop and change too. In an inner way, however, the development does not displace the value accorded attachments to others.[35]

Gilligan elaborates upon the differences she found in her research:

> In young adulthood, when identity and intimacy converge in dilemmas of conflicting commitment, the relationship between self and other is exposed. That this relationship differs in the experience of men and women is a steady theme in the literature on human development and a finding of my research. From the different dynamics of separation and attachment in their gender identity formation through the di-

vergence of identity and intimacy that marks their
experience in the adolescent years, male and female
voices typically speak of the importance of different
truths, the former of the role of separation as it defines and empowers the self, the latter of the ongoing
process of attachment that creates and sustains the
human community.[36]

Everyone needs relationships, no one can develop in a vac-
uum. Nonetheless, the dominant image of human development
is one which places relationships in a secondary role. It also
makes women the caretakers of relationships in the culture.
They are the ones who are responsible for maintaining and nur-
turing human connections. The individualism and its concomitant alienation which are so prevalent in our society are clear
signs of inadequacy of such a system.[37] Men "achieve" and are
lonely; women sacrifice "achievement" (and often selves) in the
effort to sustain relationships. Men seek relationships too late;
women, devastated when relationships are broken, are often
viewed as neurotic.

The recovery of the prime importance of relationships in the
development of all human beings is a vital factor in healing
many of the ills of our society, particularly in the area of war-
making. Assertion of oneself as against the world in search for
one's identity leads to aggression and violence. If one's value
(and very self) is defined in terms of achievement, then nothing
must stand in the way of that achievement. Baker Miller graphically describes this tendency when she writes: "We have
reached the end of the road that is built on the set of traits held
out for male identity — advance at any cost, pay any price, drive
out all competitors, and kill them if necessary."[38] An abiding
concern with maintaining relationships, with being connected
to others, results not in the destruction of those who would
threaten our "advance," but rather in what Gilligan has called
an "ethic of care and responsibility." Such an ethic is conscious
of differences and of needs, of the interconnectedness of human

beings. It "rests on the premise of nonviolence — that no one should be hurt."[39] Such an ethic finds ways other than war to resolve differences. A world view focused on interrelatedness and interdependence as primary, values life above achievement and persons over positions. It not only values these, but actively seeks to promote them.

"Enemies" take on a new meaning within this context. Gilligan notes that the women in her studies consistently asked for more details about the men and women in the examples given them. They displayed a tendency to concretize the hypothetical case studies they were given, and to place them within a human context. This same tendency is present among the women active in peace movements throughout the world. Stereotypes hold little sway when real people are the focus of attention. While stereotypes function by robbing people of their actual humanity, a relationship-oriented perspective will not allow that humanity to be denied. Enemies serve a purpose in that they allow us to define and defend ourselves against them. If, however, we grow by connectedness, our need for enemies diminishes. One seeks to affiliate with others rather than destroy them.

Relationship and networking are key to women's growth. They are also key to peacemaking. There will never be peace in our world as long as peoples view themselves as against each other. Only when they are enabled to reach out to each other, to celebrate the richness of the human reality in all of its manifestations, will the hope of a secure future begin to appear. This can only happen when we own and cherish the fundamental need we have for each other — not a need for services or for commodities or for dominating power — but a need simply for other human beings. Nuclear terror finds alleviation in our sharing its pain with each other. Nuclear war becomes far less likely in a world where "the other" is no longer the inferior, the subordinate, the enemy, but is rather the gift. What we *could* be — that other image in the mirror — is profoundly affected by the way in which we seek to grow and mature. What we could be — caring, tolerant persons who seek connection with each other — promises a future for our planet. Conversion is necessary to move from what we are to what we could be . . . conversion for both men and women. For men, it demands a re-evaluation of previously accepted images of growth, an open acknowledgement of the incompleteness of the rugged individual. For women, it demands claiming what they have always known, perhaps, but never trusted, and claiming it for themselves.

Even a brief overview of language, logic, power, and relationship from the perspective of feminist studies reveals a strikingly different world view from that proposed in the "real" male-dominated world. Language is inclusive, imaginative and celebratory of the feminine. Logic is expanded beyond the limited (and dangerous) horizon of abstract, objective rationality to include creation, imagination and vision. Power is not domination, control, power-over, but rather energy which grows in relation, which enables and empowers others. Relationship is fundamental to development, enables caring, and dissipates the need for enemies.

Peacemaking, a requirement of our faith, demands a conversion which reaches to the depths of our being even as it reaches out to encompass all aspects of our life in this our threatened world. This conversion, as I have tried to show, leads us to look into our communal mirror, to see there the rather harsh reality of who we are today, and to glimpse who we could be were we to find the courage of conversion. The facts of the nuclear reality are frightening, the costs of living in a world filled with nuclear weapons are overwhelming and strike terror in the hearts of all conscious persons.

These weapons will not disappear until we begin to recognize the world views and the patterns of behavior which make their existence not only possible but logical. Such recognition has come to us in large part as a consequence of a growing movement among women and men, a movement which seeks not merely to give women their due, but also (and more importantly) to transform the culture itself. This transformation, which involves the appropriation of values and attitudes long denied, offers hope in the face of global despair because it necessarily implies a movement away from those attitudes and values which make for war. There is light, then, in our mirror, not only for women but for all peoples.

For a believer, however, this light is not yet enough. Cultural transformation, necessary as it is, is not the whole of conversion. The call to conversion is always spoken by God's Spirit. No matter what the tone or language, the voice is always that of the Spirit, calling us to life and to clearer vision. Conversion to peacemaking is conversion in/of God's Spirit. It is movement toward blessedness (Mt 5:9) and, as such, it leads us into the reign of God, perhaps to the very heart of our God. The next two chapters attempt to articulate that movement in terms of the Judaeo-Christian biblical tradition (Chapter Five) and the imperfect, always somewhat distorted vision of the God who creates and sustains peace (Chapter Six).

5
"Seek Peace and Pursue It"
BIBLICAL ALTERNATIVE

Many images of women have been evoked thus far in this writing: women at arms bazaars, women survivors of torture, mothers of the disappeared. I would turn now to yet another image, one very ancient and yet new each time anyone, woman or man, seems to have exhausted all conventional sources of help and still knows the self to be in need. A certain daring comes to one whose need continues beyond any acceptable limit; people begin to do and say things which are somewhat unconventional. They parade in dangerous plazas, they talk about and write about their most painful experiences, they say unseemly things and make wild suggestions. Born from their suffering is a determination to find a cure, to be themselves a part of the healing.

The early Christian communities remembered such a one — a menstruating woman. All three synoptic gospels tell her story (Mt 9:20-22; Mk 5:25-34; Lk 8:43-48). Suffering from an infirmity which made her not only unhealthy but also unclean, this woman had apparently tried the conventional approaches to healing. The gospel of Mark tells us that she "had suffered much under many physicians, and had spent all that she had, and was no better but rather grew worse" (Mk 9:26).[1] In her great need, she sought out one who had healed others and who could — she believed — help her. She approached, hoping only to touch his clothing: "For she said,'If I touch even his garments, I shall be made well' "(Mk 9:28). And she was. Her act of daring and of belief enabled this heretofore unclean woman to brave crowds where she would be unwelcome, to reach out, to touch a man in public (an unacceptable action for any woman), to encounter her Savior and hear his word of peace to her. Hoping only to touch his garment, she met with the exquisite sensitivity of Jesus who felt her touch and the power-filled connection between him and herself. Healed yet still frightened, she spoke the truth to him and received blessing in return.

I believe this woman stands as symbol for all of us who have long struggled to find a healing to the disease of our time. Like her, we have tried conventional means; some of us have spent all that we had, we have consulted the doctors, the experts and the leaders, all to no avail. We now find ourselves needy and willing to go places where we are not accepted, longing for help in ending the long suffering of our peoples. Like this woman, many of us have had to live with being ostracized, labelled disloyal or merely naive. Like her, we too suspect that somehow God is involved in all of this, that some way God must be approached if we would know healing. Like her, finally, we may only touch the garment of God, or even its very fringe. Perhaps that is all that any believer ever does. But it is enough, it seems, to bring about wholeness and peace.

There are as many ways to approach God as there are human hearts, for even as we approach, our God comes to meet us. Grace greets us in each moment and in each experience of our lives, if we but attend to it. A particularly beautiful and challenging "place" of grace for us is that of the Judeo-Christian biblical tradition. The scriptures speak to us of God and of God's relationship to us and our world. They have always been revered as source of revelation: one which provides us with a glimpse of the divine as God is recognized in the history of a people, as well as a vision of the people themselves as they reflect their own self-understanding within that history. The scriptures also offer us a view of ourselves in our response not only to the words of a text but also to the experience expressed therein. How do we, for example, see our own lives in relation to those of God's people? Or do our experiences differ from theirs? Often the exterior circumstances of life change, but the deeper, fundamental questions remain the same — especially those of the presence/action of the divine in the midst of human life. The peoples of the scriptural tradition never knew about nuclear terror, but they obviously knew their own kinds of terror. They also knew of war and of a longing for peace. The texts before us reflect not only these experiences but also the people's attempts to articulate how and when they recognized the divine at the heart of it all.

The perspective of recognition is fundamental to our understanding of the scriptures, for they are, in a very real sense, a record of such recognition. They are not merely historical records but rather a form of anamnesis: a Spirit-filled remembering which has significance for the present. The writers of the texts which we call sacred and the communities in which these texts were formed told the great stories of their past time and time again. They did so out of praise for the God who had acted to save them, who had created them as a people, who sustained them. They told these stories, however, in light of the situations, the questions and struggles of their own times. The Exodus event is frequently recalled and retold in the Hebrew scriptures; not simply because it was a crucial event in the history of Israel, but also because it gave hope to a people who found themselves once again in slavery. "God has saved us before; surely God will save again," becomes the message and meaning of a past action for a people hoping once again for the salvation of their God. The gospels are also anamnesis. They are not merely accounts of the life and ministry of Jesus Christ; they are also the early Christian communities' attempts to find guidance and strength for their own struggles in the message and memory of this Jesus.

When, then, we ask of meanings of war, of peace, of peacemaking as they are shown to us in scripture, we must ask not only what the texts themselves say, but also what they show us of the perspectives of the writers and of the communities. What were their questions, and how do they relate to ours? We must, finally, allow the scriptures to question us, for revelation is always question even before it is answer.

Holy War and Shalom

At first glance, the Hebrew scriptures seem a strange place to look for peace. One could view almost the entire history of the people of Israel as a history of war. The entire book of Joshua is a recounting of the wars which took place during the Exodus and which preceded the entrance into the Promised Land. The very ancient text of Joshua 24, which recounts the covenant ceremony at Shechem previous to entrance into the land, states "And you went over the Jordan and came to Jericho, and the men of Jericho fought against you, and also the Amorites, the Perizzites, the Canaanites, the Hittites, the Girgashites, the Hivites, and the Jebusites; and I gave them into your hand" (Jos 24:11).

The battles did not end with Joshua, however. The whole period of the monarchy was plagued by war. Saul fought against the Ammonites (1 Sam 11) and the Philistines (1 Sam 13), among others. David proved his greatness when he defeated Goliath, the Philistine giant (1 Sam 17), and incurred the enmity of Saul who became enraged when ". . . the women sang to one another as they made merry, 'Saul has slain his thousands, and David his ten thousands' " (1 Sam 18:7). War between rival kings raged when the surrounding enemies were subdued. Thus, "There was a long war between the house of Saul and the house of David, and David grew stronger and stronger, while the house of Saul became weaker and weaker" (2 Sam 3:1).

After the death of Saul, David in his turn defeats the Philistines, Moabites, Aramaeans, Ammonites, Amalekites, and the Edomites — to name a few (2 Sam 8). When Israel is sundered by schism (c. 931 b.c.e.), both the northern kingdom of Israel and the southern Judah live through wars and eventually are destroyed by foreign nations: Israel in 721 by the Assyrians, Judah in 598 by the Babylonians. The wars, conquests, and battles continued into the Christian era, when Rome controlled Jerusalem and movements of revolt abounded.

The history of God's chosen people as given to us in the Hebrew scriptures is one marked by bloodshed and by war. Even more disconcerting than the innumerable wars, however, is the way the divine presence is depicted in relation to them. God is clearly involved as one who leads the armies, who guarantees victory, who gives the "spoils of war" to Israel. Deuteronomy 20 lists the rules for waging of the holy war and makes it clear that the war is led by God, won by God.

> Hear, O Israel, you draw near this day to battle against your enemies; let not your heart faint; do not fear, or tremble, or be in dread of them; for the Lord your God is he that goes with you, to fight for you against your enemies, to give you the victory' . . . and when the Lord your God gives it [the enemy] into your hand you shall put all its males to the sword, but the women and the little ones, the cattle, and everything else in the city, all its spoil, you shall take as booty for yourselves; and you shall enjoy the spoil of your enemies, which the Lord your God has given you (Deut 20:3-4, 13-14).

The Covenant Code in Ex 20:22 — 23:33 concludes with the promise that God will enable the Israelites to defeat all of their enemies. Promising an angel who will lead them, God is said to declare: "When my angel goes before you, and brings you in to the Amorites, and the Hittites, and the Perizzites, and the Canaanites, the Hivites, and the Jebusites, and I blot them out . . ." (Ex 23:23). God, then, is portrayed as the one who leads the holy war, who enables victory, who even "blots out" the enemies.

In other texts it is the Israelites who are to be defeated, and again God is involved — on the side of the enemies. The prophets speak of a God who uses other nations to overcome the unfaithful Israel. Isaiah declares that Assyria is the rod of God's anger, the staff of God's fury. He continues: "Against a godless nation I send him, and against the people of my wrath I command him, to take spoil and seize plunder, and to tread them down like the mire of the streets" (Is 10:6). Jeremiah portrays the destruction of Judah at the hands of the avenger from the north (Babylon), and even as he predicts this disaster he grieves over it. "My anguish, my anguish! I writhe in pain! Oh, the walls of my heart! My heart is beating wildly; I cannot keep silent; for I hear the sound of the trumpet, the alarm of war. Disaster follows hard on disaster, the whole land is laid waste" (Jer 4:19-20).

In still other cases, God declares war, using kings or nations as vehicles for the revelation of the power of God. Chapters 38-39 of Ezekiel tell of Gog of Magog whom God inspires to go to war against Israel. Gog is used by God in order that the divine greatness and holiness might be made manifest. "In the latter days I will bring you against my land, that the nations may know me, when through you, O Gog, I vindicate my holiness before their eyes" (Ezek 38:16). The prophet Joel speaks of a God who declares war in order to punish all of the nations that mistreated Judah. "Proclaim this among the nations: Prepare war, stir up the mighty men. Let all the men of war draw near, let them come up. Beat your plowshares into swords, and your pruning hooks into spears; let the weak say, 'I am a warrior' " (Joel 3:9-10).

Are we then to understand the God of the Judeo-Christian tradition as a warrior God, one who leads in battle, who gives detailed prescriptions as to the conduct of war, who declares war, uses war to show his greatness or to punish his own people? Are we, further, to take that next step which so many have taken throughout history and to view war as somehow holy, as something either guided by God for our salvation or for the punishment of our sins? To answer these questions it is necessary to look somewhat deeper into the text and to seek there the way in which war imagery is used in order to make theological statements.

The authors of the Hebrew scriptures as well as the editors and collators who followed them were not historians but rather theologians. That is, they viewed their history as the context in which God acted and called them to certain responses. They used many images and metaphors to make their points and retold their history in ways which made its theological content explicit. The Exodus was not primarily seen as the history of Israel's escape from Egypt or its wandering through the desert for forty years. Rather, it was the story of God's freeing the Israelites from their slavery in Egypt and of God's punishing an unfaithful people by delaying their entrance into the promised land, even as the divine presence enabled their continued existence during that time.

Wars did happen frequently in the history of God's people, but it was the authors of the scriptures who gave them a religious significance in order to make a theological statement. In some cases, an anticipated war was an image for God's punishment of a people unfaithful to the covenant. This is particularly true of the prophets' use of war imagery.[2] Isaiah and Jeremiah both summon up images of war and defeat in order to threaten those who are unfaithful and unjust. Immediately before Isaiah declares that Assyria is "the rod of my [God's] anger," he cries: "Woe to those who decree iniquitous decrees, and the writers who keep writing oppression, to turn aside the needy from justice, and to rob the poor of my people of their right, that widows may be their spoil, and that they may make the fatherless their prey!" (Is 10:1-2). Jeremiah predicts the terrible devastation to be wreaked upon Judah because they are a faithless people, foolish and childish who "are skilled in doing evil, but how to do good they know not" (Jer 4:22).

Hosea tells the people of Israel that "the tumult of war shall arise among your people," because they have "plowed iniquity and reaped injustice. . . . Because you have trusted in your chariots and in the multitude of your warriors" (Hos 10:13-14). What is important to these prophets is the infidelity of their people, especially as that infidelity is manifested in injustice and oppression of the poor. God will surely punish those who do injustice, who lay burdens upon the weak. War is the image used to portray the devastation of this judgment and to urge the people toward conversion.

Even as the prophets promise devastation to an unfaithful people, they always remind them of the faithful God who, even in their sin and misery, will not abandon them totally. There is promise of a remnant who will return from captivity (Is 10:20, for example). There are images of a converted Israel who will at last be faithful to God (Hos 2:14-23 is a classic example of this type of imagery). There is the promise of a new, more perfect covenant as in Jer 31:31-34. *And* there is the image of a war wherein God will vindicate those who have made Israel suffer. Ezekiel, in exile with his people, seeks to console them and to remind them of God's fidelity. He paints a picture of a war whose outcome will be the restoration of Israel to the promised land. Still later, during the Persian reign over Judah, Joel draws an image of such a war within the context of the "day of the Lord," an eschatological "day" when God's judgment will be made visible and the Lord will "restore the fortunes of Judah and Jerusalem" (Joel 3:1).

War, then, is often used as an image for the punishment of the unjust or the restoration of the suffering. The fidelity/infidelity of God's people (and especially the leaders of the people) was the primary focus of the Deuteronomists in their retelling of wars long past.[3] These writers and editors of historical narratives were intensely concerned with the danger of idolatry and inveighed heavily against any possible contamination by "foreign elements" which might lead Israel into such idolatry.

They portray the history of the Conquest in terms of the people's fidelity/idolatry. When/if Israel was faithful, God enabled them to win wars. When unfaithful, they were defeated.

Often idolatry itself is seen as the cause of a war. The downfall of both Israel and Judah are portrayed as punishment for the idolatry practiced in both kingdoms. The Deuteronomists who composed their histories in the time of exile made those histories the vehicle for their theological conviction: the absolute necessity of true worship. Their purpose was to convince the people to remain faithful to the God of Israel, to refrain from any contamination with other nations which would lead to the worship of false gods. The historical wars became image of the deeper, more significant struggle within the hearts of the people.

War was indeed a significant aspect in the history of God's people as they sought to conquer the promised land and as they sought to retain their control over that land. The Hebrew scriptures, however, have transformed the concrete historical reality into a religious metaphor which speaks not of the value of war and warriors but of the demand for fidelity to God and of the dire consequences of infidelity.

A further point must be stated concerning the use of war as metaphor in the Hebrew scriptures. These scriptures are the story of the Patriarchs, written by men and mostly about men. Like all such histories, they betray a tendency to glorify what are so often seen as the masculine virtues: strength, prowess in battle, leadership of armies, defeating the enemies. It is perhaps significant to note that even the stories of women such as Deborah, Esther, and Judith deal with the slaying of the enemy. Judith, for example, is praised after the killing of Holofernes and so is the God "who created the heavens and the earth, who has guided you to strike the head of the leader of our enemies" (Judith 13:19). One can only wonder how these stories would have been told if their authors had been women.

The Hebrew scriptures are not only about war, however. Peace, *shalom,* is also present. *Shalom* can appear as a vague wish or a temporary truce between two warring factions. In other places, *shalom* seems to be a salutation, a common expression much like our "hello" or "goodbye." The meaning of *shalom,* however, is much broader and more significant than any single term can convey, and all manifestations of peace — from the mundane to the miraculous — are interrelated. All somehow reflect the mystery which is the *shalom* of God. The peace spoken of in the Hebrew scriptures is multifaceted and profoundly rich. *Shalom* is a metaphor which represents a longed-for reality and which evokes both belief and hope in the God of Israel. It also often convicts the people even as it calls them to conversion, especially conversion to hope. In its most basic sense, *shalom* speaks of a wondrous harmony which reaches from an individual's heart to relations between persons and nations and to all of creation.[4] This harmony begins and ends in the heart of God, the giver and maker of *shalom.* It encompasses all areas of life and is the name for eschatological fullness.

Different texts, arising from different historical circumstances and specific theological orientations, stress different aspects of biblical peace. Prophets writing before the downfall of Israel and Judah refer to peace within the context of calls to conversion. Those writing during exile, on the other hand, stress peace as integral to the nation's hope. Throughout the Hebrew scriptures, however, *shalom* is present. It is prayed for in blessings; it is elemental to worship of the creator and savior God; it is hoped for in visions of the messianic time, and its lack is judgment on an unfaithful Israel. In order to even glimpse the richness of *shalom,* it is necessary to look briefly at its many uses and multiple meanings.

In the first place, true peace is of God and is related to God's merciful love for the people; God alone gives peace or takes it away. The prophets say this repeatedly. They berate an unfaithful people from whom God has taken peace away: "for I have

taken away my peace from this people, says the Lord, my steadfast love and mercy" (Jer 16:5) and maintain that God keeps the
faithful one in peace (Is 26:3). The psalms praise the God who
makes peace in Israel (Ps 147:14) and pray to that God to bless
the people with peace (29:11). The beautiful and oft-quoted blessing in Numbers 6:26 concludes with the prayer that God will
look upon the people "and give you peace." *Shalom,* then, ema-
nates from the goodness of God and is manifestation of the good
God's love and blessing for a people.

Secondly, *shalom* always implies relationship, and this relationship has three aspects. It is relationship between God and
the people, among the people themselves, between the people
and all creation. The possibility of peace resides in the actuality
of covenant. All of Hebrew scriptures witness to the belief that
God had chosen to enter into a profound and intimate relationship with a people who neither deserved this gift nor cherished
it as they should. God as the giver of peace is always seen as God-
in-relationship. Because Israel is allowed to know this God, she
is able to know God's peace. When the relationship flourishes,
peace is present. When it does not, peace dies. Thus Israel's holy
ones often connect fidelity and peace. Second Isaiah, for example, laments that Israel did not obey the commandments of God,
for if they had, their peace would have been like a river (Is
48:18).

To be in covenant with God demands that the people's lives
manifest that they truly do belong to the faithful, merciful God.
The quality of relationships within the community reflect the
intensity with which covenant is kept. In this respect, *shalom* is
intimately linked to justice and is even synonymous with it.
When justice flourishes among the people, peace is present; but
when injustice is done, there is no peace. God's people are called
to merciful, compassionate fidelity to each other. They must be
particularly sensitive to those among them who are most needy,
most helpless. If they do not know this kind of justice among
themselves, they will not know peace. "The way of peace they

know not, and there is no justice in their paths; they have made their roads crooked, and no one who goes in them knows peace" (Is 59:8). The prophets are particularly harsh with those who would deny this connection, and they rail against the false prophets who claim there is peace when in fact there is not (Jer 6:14; 14:13; Ezek 13:10,16). *Shalom* as gift means, therefore, *shalom* as activity.

While relationships within the community are essential to knowing peace, God's peace is not to be seen as limited to one people. It is, rather, a harmony and fruitful union which extends to other nations and to all of creation. When the people learn to walk in God's ways, God will "decide for many peoples; and they shall beat their swords into plowshares, and their spears into pruning hooks; nation shall not lift up sword against nation, neither shall they learn war any more" (Is 2:4). Nations will not be at war and all of creation will rejoice together. The reign of peace will encompass all of creation. Natural enemies will dwell together in harmony; children will play safely at the snake's den, the wolf and the lamb will be together, and "they shall not hurt or destroy in all my holy mountain" (Is 11:6-9).

Finally, peace is fundamental to the eschatological hope of Israel, and here it becomes practically synoymous with salvation as in the magnificent description of God's salvation in Ps 85: "Steadfast love and faithfulness will meet; righteousness and peace will kiss each other. Faithfulness will spring up from the ground, and righteousness will look down from the sky" (vv. 10-11).

Even a brief look at the war-filled history of the people of God has made it abundantly clear that wars did not cease, the fulfillment of Israel's hopes did not arrive. Because of this,the longing for the fulness of God's reign became more and more intense, and the images used to describe that reign became more vivid. One of the key images is that of a new covenant. Even though they had been unfaithful and had broken covenant repeatedly, a time would come when God would make a new, even

more intimate bonding with the people. The prophets promise
this and frequently describe it as a covenant of peace:"My covenant of peace shall not be removed, says the Lord who has compassion on you;" "I will make a covenant of peace with them; it
shall be an everlasting covenant with them; and I will bless
them and multiply them, and will set my sanctuary in the midst
of them for evermore" (Is 54:10; Ezek 37:26; 34:25). Perhaps
Hosea describes this blessed time best in his portrayal of a converted Israel:

> And I will make for you a covenant on that day with
> the beasts of the field, the birds of the air, and the
> creeping things of the ground; and I will abolish the
> bow, the sword, and war from the land; and I will
> make you lie down in safety. And I will betroth you to
> me for ever; I will betroth you to me in righteousness
> and in justice, in steadfast love, and in mercy. I will
> betroth you to me in faithfulness; and you shall know
> the Lord. And in that day, says the Lord, I will answer
> the heavens and they shall answer the earth; and the
> earth shall answer the grain, the wine, and the oil, .
> . . (Hos 2:18-22)

The eschatological hope for peace eventually was joined
with the hope for a Messiah who would come to Israel and restore her to wholeness. This One, frequently seen as of the line
of David, would shepherd the people, establish justice among
them, and bring peace. He would be called "Wonderful Coun-
selor, Mighty God, Everlasting Father, Prince of Peace" (Is 9:6).
For Micah, the Messiah will come from Bethlehem, he will give
the people security, "and this shall be peace" (5:4-6); and an ora-
cle in Zechariah promises that "the battle bow shall be cut off,
and he shall command peace to the nations" (9:9-10).

Gift and blessing of a merciful God, promise to a people
called to live in justice, hope of these same people, *shalom* lies at
the very heart of Israel's belief. The pursuit of peace — "Seek

peace and pursue it" (Ps 34:14) — is essential to her story. This story is one of a people who viewed themselves as beset by foes at every stage in their history, as followers of great leaders, as woeful captives of villainous invaders, as strong warriors at times and unfaithful sinners at others. Always within this story is the conviction and the memory and the teaching that this people — of all peoples on the earth — had been chosen by the one true God. This God, their God, entered into covenant with them and stayed with them always, even in and through their infidelity. Theirs was a God who could not give them up (Hos 11:1-3), even though sorely tried. Theirs was a God who kept the promise, and central to the promise was peace. Peace meant more than the defeat of their enemies, other than prosperity, and more than national security. God's peace meant harmony and wholeness, goodness and justice, true relationships, creation in unity. *Shalom* would appear when salvation took place, and it would make people unafraid.

Israel knew that this wondrous time had not yet arrived; she knew, too, that *it would come,* and that its coming would be heralded by the arrival of the Messiah, the savior, the Prince of Peace. It was theirs to wait and to hope, to wait actively and to hasten the day by their own truth to covenant, their own conversion to *shalom.*

Shalom and holy war as they are presented in the Hebrew scriptures are complex metaphors; wide in scope, rich in meaning, they challenge us, inspire us, and often perplex us. They tell us some important things, I believe. Peace is more than negotiations and treaties, it is other than superpower weapons. Peace is of God, and it is God's will for us and for all of creation. Enmity and war are not "normal" for the believer, and the pursuit of peace cannot be left to others. This pursuit is the call of all who profess belief in a faithful God. It implies the establishment and nurturance of true, just relationships. It demands radical conversion, perhaps especially a conversion to hope. In these times of terror, it is crucial to remember that our God is indeed faithful and does keep the promise. Peace is the destiny of God's people. As such, it is our duty now to live toward that destiny confident that God will not betray us, conscious of our responsibility to cooperate in the promise.

Finally, there are three particular subthemes which emerge in even a brief review of the sacred texts which need special but brief mention: idolatry, justice, creation.

We have seen that much of the war imagery of the Hebrew scriptures served as a vehicle for the condemnation of idolatry. War was holy when it aimed at keeping God's people from the worship of false gods; it was inevitable punishment when the people were guilty of such worship. While it is simplistic — and incorrect interpretation — to view winners and losers in wars as either holy or sinners, it behooves us, I believe, to listen carefully to the serious warnings against idolatry which are contained in these metaphors. There are many types of idolatry among us, and they work against peace. In the first place, the weapons themselves can (and have) become the objects of a subtle form of worship. The great power of nuclear weapons, the "mightiness" of a nuclear explosion, the sense we have that these weapons are somehow beyond our control all serve to lead people to trust in the weapons themselves and to look to nuclear weapons for our salvation. It is the weapons which will save us in war, which protect us now. National security is equated with numbers, sizes, types of nuclear weapons. This current image of security differs radically from that of a people who rest securely because all of creation is in harmony. Can security ever be equated with destruction? Have we turned from the true God to one made with human hands? And, in so doing, have we turned from life to death?

There is another even more subtle tendency to idolatry which is consistently present among human beings, that of making God in our image. The valued traits and characteristics of a given culture find themselves mirrored in that culture's representation of the divine. In white, western culture, for example, the divine is usually portrayed as Caucasian and in the case of Jesus Christ, as fairhaired and blue-eyed. More significantly, God has been named as "He," as "Father," and "His" might and power and domination of all that exists have been extolled. This God is rational (how often we refer to the God*head*), "He" rewards the good and punishes the evil, even as we must. Even today, God all too often is all of the things that make for a good soldier.

But this is not all of the truth of God. No single image, no set of images can convey the wholeness of the divine. It is we who are made in God's image, not God who is made in ours. God is always beyond us; our attempts to understand are always those of the woman who only reached for the hem of the garment. God forms and shapes us, we do not form God. It is not for us, then, nor for any dominant group within a culture to presume that what we value and honor is what God values or honors. We veer dangerously close to idolatry when we assume that we know all of God and that this God is a reflection of our accepted cultural values. If we accept the fact that so many of these values are ones which make for war, then we must recognize that we are in danger of recreating the Warrior God and of using that God for our own purposes.

The Hebrew scriptures make it evident that *shalom* cannot live unless justice prevails. There is no peace in the midst of injustice. One cannot work for peace without also working for justice. What is crucial here, I feel, is the *kind* of justice that the Hebrew scriptures present. The justice which is demanded is not that of "fairness" or equal representation under the law. It is neither logical nor impartial. Justice in covenant is merciful justice marked by caring and by compassion, and it reaches quickly and surely to those who most need it. This justice does not allow for the domination of one group over another, nor can it rest until all persons are brought to wholeness. In a time of psychic numbing, amidst a culture which values fairness and logic and places such great trust in laws, the Hebrew scriptures remind us that peacemaking demands care, compassion and attentiveness to the needy among us. We are not allowed to escape the suffering of our times, nor can we live without a gracious mercy which reaches out to others not because they deserve it, but simply because they are.

Finally, these scriptures remind us that peace involves all of creation. Not only shall people live in peace with each other, they shall also be at peace with creation. This fact serves to remind us of our responsibility to/for the created world. Not only are we of the earth, we are also called to care for the earth, tend it, protect it, cherish it as gift. Peacemaking is duty for all creatures, for it is terrible arrogance and true blasphemy to allow the destruction of creation by the created in defiance of the Creator who has called this earth good.

Blessed are the Peacemakers

While the Hebrew scriptures present us with questions and with inspiration in our search for the meaning and making of peace, they are not our only Word. For Christians, there is yet another source which flows from the Hebrew scriptures but speaks from the conviction that God has brought them to fulfilment in the person, message, ministry of Jesus who is the Christ. What do the Christian scriptures, the memories and struggles of the early Christians tell us about peace and peacemaking? What do they show us of the one who "is our peace" (Eph 2:14)?

The early Christian communities believed that God's reign had been inaugurated in the life-death-resurrection of Jesus. They viewed themselves as members of the new people of God and as living within the eschatological age, the "now" of salvation. Integral to that salvation was peace. Thus, the followers of Jesus preached "the good news of peace by Jesus Christ" (Acts 10:36) and urged each other to seek peace (Heb 12:14) and to aim at peace (2 Tim 2:22). As with *shalom* in the Hebrew scriptures, peace in the New Testament has many aspects and relates to all areas of life. Unlike the Hebrew scriptures, however, this peace has been accomplished through the reconciliation achieved by Jesus Christ.

Reconciliation in the New Testament is primarily one between God and humankind. It is achieved in the forgiveness and salvation effected by Jesus the Christ. Paul describes it as an effect of justification and declares in 2 Corinthians that "in Christ God was reconciling the world to himself, not counting their trespasses against them" (5:19; see also Rom 5:10). This reconciliation gives the believer access to grace, it restores the relationship between God and God's people, it makes for peace. "Therefore, since we are justified by faith, we have peace with God through our Lord Jesus Christ. Through him we have obtained access to this grace in which we stand, and we rejoice in our hope of sharing the glory of God" (Rom 5:1-2).

The centrality of Jesus Christ to the establishment of peace is developed in the letters to the Colossians and the Ephesians. Colossians contains a great hymn of praise of Jesus (1:15-23), and within this hymn we are told that Jesus' reconciliation extends to "all things, whether on earth or in heaven" (1:20). Jesus has made peace by "the blood of his cross."[5] In his fidelity to God's reign and his willingness to give his life, all creation enters into salvation. Ephesians tells us that in Jesus all people have access to God. In his very person, Jesus has broken down the walls of hostility which had existed for so very long. Not only is all creation reconciled, all persons are too. The division between Jew and Gentile ceases to exist; those who were far off "have been brought near to God in the blood of Christ" (Eph 2:13; see also Gal 3:28).

As the Hebrew scriptures reflect a belief that peace with God was unattainable without justice among the people, so too the New Testament insists that since we have been reconciled to God there must be peace within the community. Ephesians urges the community to lead a life "worthy of the calling to which

you have been called," and to be "eager to maintain the unity of
the Spirit in the bond of peace" (Eph 4:1-3). Paul urges the communities of Romans, Corinthians, and Thessalonians (Rom
12:18; 1 Cor 7:15; 14:33; 2 Cor 13:11; 1Thess 5:13) to live together in peace. He consistently decries any divisions which appear among any of the early Christians. God has made us one,
he cries, how can we be divided?

Peace, established in Jesus Christ, expressed in unity
within the community, is clearly the gift of God. God is frequently called the "God of Peace" in the New Testament letters
(Rom 15:33; 16:20; 2 Cor 13:11; Phil 4:9; 2 Thess 3:16; Heb
13:20), and God's peace, "which passes all understanding," sustains the believers (Phil 4:7; see also Col 3:15 where Christ's
peace is to rule in the hearts of the people). "Harvest of righteousness" (Jas 3:18), peace is gift of the Spirit (Gal 5:22) and
sign of the kingdom (Rom 14:17).

The gospels relate peace to the kingdom and the kingdom-
bringer. In Luke's gospel the arrival of Jesus is also the arrival
of peace. After the birth of John the Baptist, Luke tells us that
Zachariah "was filled with the Holy Spirit" and prophesied concerning the one who would go before the Lord to prepare the
way. The canticle of Zachariah (Lk 1:67-79), relying heavily
upon citations from the Hebrew scriptures, speaks of the coming
of God's reign. It sings of the knowledge of salvation, the forgiveness of sin "through the tender mercy of our God," the light
which shall shine on those who sit in darkness, the call of John
to "guide our feet into the way of peace." The heavenly host
which announces the birth of the Messiah gives glory to God and
declares peace among those with whom God is pleased (2:14). Si-
meon, who had been promised he would not see death until he
had seen the Christ, declares that now he can depart in peace
because he has seen the salvation of the people (2:29). When
Jesus enters Jerusalem in triumph, the people, echoing the
angels' song cry out: "Blessed is the King who comes in the name
of the Lord! Peace in heaven and glory in the highest"(19:38).[6]

Shortly after this, Jesus weeps over Jerusalem because it did not know "the things that make for peace" (19:42). It did not recognize the Messiah. To recognize the Christ is to encounter peace. Belief and peace are closely connected, therefore, as the example of the woman with the hemorrage shows. Her faith saved her, she was sent in peace (Lk 8:48; Mk 5:34).

The peace which Jesus brought was not that of the false prophets. It was, rather, like that of Jeremiah and Isaiah, a peace which rested upon justice and fidelity within the community. It was necessary for the people to repent, to believe the good news in order to enter into God's reign; Jesus never hesitated to make this very clear. Acceptance of the reign meant conversion and walking in a new way. Many were not willing to do this. For them, Jesus' message was not good news. Matthew and Luke refer to the inevitable tension created by Jesus when they portray him as declaring that he did not bring peace but rather division (Mt 10:34; Lk 12:51). This division, which reaches even to the heart of the family itself, occurs among those who can accept Jesus (and thus true peace), and those who cannot.

When the disciples are told to let their peace remain with those who accept them but to withdraw it from those who do not (Mt 10:13; Lk 9:4-5), we are once again reminded that true peace is profoundly related to acceptance of the gospel and that such acceptance must be total. The demands of the reign of God are not open to compromise. Sin is forgiven, but unacknowledged sin is not ignored. The peace of the gospel, God's peace, is a religious reality rather than merely a social one. It does not show itself in a comfortable *status quo,* but in a loving, active embrace of the reign of God.

The Gospel of John underlines the connection between peace and Jesus Christ. Peace is Jesus' farewell gift to his friends, one which enables them to be unafraid, to know joy in the midst of sorrow. The image of peace brackets the death-resurrection in this gospel. It appears in the farewell discourses (chs. 14-17) and in the resurrection appearances to the disciples (20:19, 21) and to Thomas (20:26). The farewell discourses portray a Jesus who seeks to console and strengthen his disciples, who calls them to continue to believe in him, who commands them to love one another even as he has loved them. These chapters remind us of the love of Jesus for those whom he called friends and his tender concern for those who will be tempted to despair in face of the apparent defeat of God's chosen one. Jesus and the Father will remain with the disciples, will abide in their hearts. The disciples will know this, and they will understand everything because God's Spirit will dwell with them. They will know joy in the midst of tribulation and understand that what appears to be disaster is in fact salvation. Jesus will give them the Spirit and his peace, one different from that of the world. Jesus' peace is synonymous with salvation, and it is to be found only in him as he continues to be present to those whom he loves.

This peace is not one which does not know struggle, nor is it a smugness which presumes that one is in possession of the truth and has only to wait until the less enlightened finally recognize it. It is not removed from the world of sorrow and of suffering; on the contrary, it is immersed in both. Jesus' peace is courage when courage should fail; it is joy when anguish threatens to overwhelm. It is, finally, the gift of resurrection. When the risen Christ appears in the midst of the frightened disciples, he greets them with peace and sends them forth. " 'Peace be with you. As the Father has sent me, even so I send you.' And when he had said this, he breathed on them and said to them, 'Receive the Holy Spirit' " (Jn 20:21-22). The two gifts promised before his death are now given in the resurrection. The Lucan promise of peace on earth is realized: the miracle of resurrection and the salvation to which it gives witness bring forth the true peace of God.

Peace in the New Testament, then, echoes the *shalom* of the Hebrew scriptures. It is of God and given by God, it comes to life in relationship to the merciful, saving God and expresses itself in the life of the community. Because the Christian believers recognized Jesus to be the promised Messiah, the Prince of Peace, they also recognized the arrival of eschatological peace in his presence. They knew themselves to be called both to share in this peace and to continue to make it active in their lives. As Jesus is our peace, as he has made peace in his blood, so too the disciples are to make peace — actively. The New Testament reveals a recognition that God's reign was not yet fully active in the world; it speaks an urgency to make it so. The sense of mission is intense in all of the New Testament writings. Fundamental to that mission is the making of peace among the communities themselves but also beyond that. The good news of peace must be preached, the peacemakers are blessed and are called children of God (Mt 5:9).

Matthew includes the peacemakers in his Beatitudes, and in so doing shows the importance of peace within God's reign. He also shows that the making of peace is a fundamental activity for those who seek to live within that reign, "a requirement of our faith." Jesus made peace in the blood of his cross, and his life and ministry are paradigm for any would-be peacemaker. Perhaps a brief look at Jesus' words and actions can provide further insight into what it means to "make peace" today. Language, logic, power, and relationship, so pivotal in contemporary life, were also of great significance in Jesus' life. What did they mean to him, and how are they portrayed in the gospel traditions?

Jesus and Language

The early Christian communities were convinced that Jesus' words were integral to his mission, that they were powerful and life-giving. The gospel of John portrays Jesus as the Word Incarnate (Jn 1:14), whose word calls for belief even as it offers eternal life. "Simon Peter answered him, 'Lord, to whom shall we go? You have the words of eternal life" (Jn 6:68; see also

5:24; 8:51). Jesus' word, which is truly God's word, purifies the disciples (15:3) and enables them to recognize Jesus as the one sent by God (17:7-8). It sustains the community in the midst of its suffering (17:14-18), and becomes the community's word which in turn leads others to believe (17:20).

The synoptic gospels stress the power of Jesus' words and their capacity to astonish those who hear them. "And they were astonished at his teaching, for he taught them as one who had authority, and not as the scribes" (Mk 1:22,27; Mt 7:28-29; Lk 4:32). This power healed the sick, sent demons scurrying, forgave sin, proclaimed the reign of God. His was not an uncontroversial word, it was rather one which challenged the accepted world view of his time even as it reversed the expectations of the people. "You have heard it said, . . . but I say to you . . ." (Mt 5:21-48). Jesus' language was that of the people; it was concrete, filled with images from everyday life. He did not use language to hide the truth. His whole mission was to reveal, and it is the revelatory character of his word which is most remarkable. He did not so much talk *about* the reign of God as talk *from* it. The language of Jesus is an interpretation of people's lives in terms of the kingdom. To hear Jesus was to be exposed to God's kingdom, to be invited into the mercy and forgiveness of God. To hear his word was to be forced to choose: repent and believe the good news, or walk away. "Who has ears to hear, let them hear!" (cf. Mk 4:9,23).

Nowhere is the challenging and revelatory character of Jesus' language more evident than in his use of parable. We all know that Jesus frequently taught in parable, and most of us know many of those parables by heart. They are for us delightful stories of how things happen when God is involved. The word of God grows and multiplies if we listen to it and accept it (Mk 4:3-8; and par.), the lost sheep is found (Mt 18:12-13; Lk 15:4-6), the runaway son is welcomed home (Lk 15:11-32). They seem to be simple stories with generally happy endings. Their retelling gives us hope and confidence in a merciful God. We "know" the parables.

Recent biblical scholarship has shown that most of us don't really "know" the parables. They are not nice stories at all. They are, rather, experiences of the kingdom which are shattering.[7] Parables are expanded metaphors which function by enabling the hearer to participate in the metaphor itself. What begins as a simple story of everyday reality eventually becomes an experience of God's kingdom which shatters that reality and the logic contained therein. Parables tell us that things are not as we had expected in the kingdom. They enable us to experience that unexpected, and lead us to accept it or to reject it.

A brief look at one of Jesus' parables, the Good Samaritan (Lk 10:30-35), will perhaps provide us with insight into Jesus' language as well as into the meaning of neighbors and enemies as they are in the kingdom which we claim as believers. Luke records the parable within the context of a lawyer's questions to Jesus: "What shall I do to inherit eternal life?" "Who is my neighbor?" Jesus responds by telling a story of a man who was attacked and robbed while he was on his way from Jerusalem to Jericho. Left to die in the ditch, the man is seen by a priest and a Levite, both of whom pass by and leave him in his misery. A Samaritan then sees him, helps him, takes him to an inn and sees that he gets further help. Jesus then asks the lawyer which of the three was the true neighbor. The lawyer responds, "The one who showed mercy on him" (10:37). "Go and do likewise," says Jesus.

Were this a simple story with a moral, the lesson would be obvious: we should be willing to help our neighbors in time of trouble. But parable is more than moral lesson. Something totally other happens if we hear the parable as Jesus' contemporaries did. The parable opens with a very normal occurrence. The Jericho-Jerusalem road was notoriously dangerous; it is not surprising that someone would be attacked while travelling it. The disregard of the priest and the Levite would certainly disgruntle some of Jesus' hearers, especially the priests and Levites among the group! Not all the hearers would be shocked, however, for neither were universally acclaimed heroes at that time. The hearers would now expect a third person, a good person who would help the poor victim. Enter the Samaritan who has compassion on the victim, whose care is elaborately described as going far beyond the necessary minimum. He even promises to come back and pay for any additional expenses.

With the entrance of this good Samaritan, the everydayness of the parable is interrupted and the shock of the kingdom is revealed. Samaritans were hated by the Jews and considered evil, "a hated enemy, a half-breed, a perverter of true religion."[8] Jesus tells the Jews that it is this evil one who has compassion and care for one of them while the "good" people pass by. "Which one, do you think, is the neighbor?" Will you say that those you despise are good? This is what it is like in the kingdom . . . "Let the one who has ears to hear, hear!" What will you choose? If you are convinced of your own neediness, if you identify with the victim in the ditch, you will undoubtedly choose one way. If, however, you identify with those who passed by, or you find it impossible to allow the reversal of accepted categories which happens when God reigns, you will most likely choose differently. And in the choice lies entrance into the kingdom.

Jesus' language is the language of the kingdom. It is powerful: able to heal, to still creation, to astonish and bless. It is language of the everyday world which points to the ordinary as place of God's grace among us. It is above all language which reveals, which discloses the acting of God in people's lives, in the person of Jesus. To hear this language is to be invited into the kingdom; it is also to be faced with a choice which demands that one let go of presuppositions and positions in order to be free to embrace the mercy of God. All are able to hear this language; its invitation reaches all sorts of persons. No special credentials are required, only the willingness to hear and be astonished.

Nuclear language hides and distorts. It erects barriers and hinders understanding. Nuclear language is the language of death hidden behind acronyms, euphemisms and jargon.

Feminist language, reflective of experience with invisibility, dismissal, and exclusion, evokes life and inclusion. It speaks and reveals women's experience. It goes behind and beyond the euphemisms and jargon to find the people at stake. It offers significant alternatives to deadly nuclear language. Such language is hope in a terrorized world. But it is still not enough. It is the language of the reign of God that is needed, the language which astonishes as it reveals, which forgives as it demands repentance, which acts as it is spoken, which, finally, challenges us to call enemy good even as we look into our individual and communal mirrors.

The Logic of the Kingdom

The parable of the Good Samaritan is symbolic of the logic of the kingdom as reflected in Jesus and in the gospel tradition. The gospels, particularly the synoptic gospels,[9] are not philosophical treatises about some abstract "truth." They do not show us a community in search of theory, but a people transformed by what has occurred among them. Concrete, enthralling narratives, they disclose a person and, in that person, the arrival of the reign of God.

Jesus, we are told, is recognized as a great teacher. He is; but his teaching is not that of a Socrates or a Plato. It is, rather, one which enters into the most ordinary of life and finds there God's grace. Jesus talks about flowers in fields and sparrows and the routine tasks of life such as housecleaning, wedding etiquette, or planting of seeds. He tells over and over again of the incoming of grace into *this* life to *these* persons. His call is to repent and believe the good news. What he requires is conversion of life, not intellectual brilliance. Luke 10:21 shows us a Jesus who praises God because revelation has been given to the little ones instead of the "wise and understanding." This same Jesus finds himself in tension with those who would insist upon the priority of the abstract principle and law over the needs of human persons: the daughter of Abraham who suffers has priority over the sabbath laws (Lk 13:10-16); so too the man with the withered arm (Lk 6:6-11), so too the disciples who are hungry (Lk 6:1-5). Jesus knows the law and is portrayed as able to discuss and interpret it. He has come to fulfill the law (Mt 5:17-20), and he does. This fulfillment, however, is achieved through the advent of God's mercy and forgiveness among the people who so long for it.

In Jesus, the logic of the kingdom is introduced among us. This logic subverts the accepted wisdom, transforms standard categories, and forces a radical reappraisal of all of life. Robert Funk speaks of the two logics which are involved in parables: that of the everyday world and that of the kingdom. The logic of the kingdom shatters that of the everyday world, and:

> evokes a radically new relation to reality *in its every-dayness*. The parable does not turn the auditor away from the mundane, but toward it. He [sic] discovers that his [sic] destiny is at stake precisely in his [sic] ordinary creaturely existence. By means of metaphor, the parable 'cracks' the shroud of every-dayness lying over mundane reality in order to grant a radically new vision of mundane reality.[10]

This new logic, expressed most dramatically and most mysteriously in parable, is that of blessedness for the poor, food for the hungry, joy for mourners, forgiveness and welcome for sinner and stranger. It is ultimately the logic of the cross which gives up life that all may have life, which believes in God's saving presence and power — even through death.

Jesus' logic looks not to theories or technological advances to save, it looks rather to the power of God. People are not hidden or reduced to numbers in his logic. They are the very "stuff" of it and of the kingdom. His concern for persons is of essence to the gospel, and this concern is not abstract or emotionless. The gospels reveal a Teacher unafraid of showing his emotions. He becomes angry at those who tithe and yet neglect justice, who lay burdens upon the people (Lk 11:37-54; Mt 23:1-6). He takes aggressive action against those who transform the temple from place of worship to place of commerce (Lk 19:45-46; Mt 21:12-13; Mk 11:15-19; Jn 2:13-17). He weeps over a city which will not accept him and thus does not know the ways of peace (Lk 19:41-42), and he weeps with his friends who suffer (Jn 11:35). He himself suffered: with his friends, and in his own heart.

The synoptic accounts of the passion of Jesus tell us of one who faced death and feared it. We tend to look upon the passion and death of Jesus as a sort of passing-through something. Our eyes generally focus on the glory of the resurrection, and we overlook the genuine anguish of one who knew he was about to die. He did not reason death away, offer it up for a good cause, or sacrifice his life for his principles. He died, excruciatingly so, and no part of him including his emotions was exempt from that death. The Savior, then, was not some brilliant philosopher who glided through life imparting his theoretical knowledge. He was, rather, a fully human person who lived, who told wonderful imaginative stories, who wept and who was afraid, who cared and who saved. His logic, that of the kingdom, shatters the logic of our world as it did his. It forces us — if we would hear — to redefine our categories, re-evaluate our priorities, rename our enemies. And it demands that we do so with our lives, in the mundane everyday existence. Christianity is not a textbook reality. It is flesh and blood struggle, even as it is rejoicing in the merciful God who is with us, who awaits us.

Jesus knew fear and he also talked about fear. He repeatedly told people not to be afraid often in the most frightening circumstances: before his death, for instance, or on a stormy sea. He also told his disciples not to be afraid of what others will say, nor of the inevitable persecution they must face (Mt 10:20, 26-33). "Fear not, little flock, for it is your Father's good pleasure to give you the kingdom" (Lk 12:32). These admonitions must have meant a great deal to the early communities when they found themselves troubled, exposed to rejection, threatened with persecution. They are also meaningful to us.

Jesus' call to put away fear is not an invitation to escape from the world or to deny the very real terror that stalks us and our planet. It is rather a word of courage in the very midst of that terror. One need not be afraid because there is courage and strength to be found in the kingdom, in closeness to the one who remains with the believers. The Hebrew scriptures associate eschatological peace with true security which is of God. The gospels manifest a security which is also of God, which rests in trust and faithful following of the Word, which endures in the continuing grace which is the gospel. But this security is found in the midst of insecurity and of the ever-present surprise and paradox of God's reign. The peacemaker as disciple is not to be afraid, for she/he touches the security of God. At the same time, she/he must never be deluded by a false security which places absolute trust in any other entity. J.D. Crossan poses the question succinctly: "Can we walk and act in utter serenity and in utter insecurity, in total concern and in total incertitude?"[11]

Nuclear logic glorifies theories and abstract rationalism. It denies persons, emotions, and reality. Feminist logic remains open to imagination, intuition, emotions and persons. It professes that there is more to truth than facts, more to the human person than the head. The logic of the kingdom made visible in Jesus shows us that God always remains mystery, that imagination and emotion are elemental to salvation, that persons in their everyday lives are the very heart of the kingdom. This "logic" calls us to courage and warns of complacency. *This* logic is grace.

The Power of Jesus

When the woman with the hemorrage found the courage to reach out in the midst of a crowd of people and touch the hem of Jesus' garment, she was healed; and, we are told, Jesus felt "that power had gone forth from him" (Mk 5:30). That Jesus possessed an extraordinary power cannot be disputed. The gospels frequently refer to his power and authority. These were unlike any other the people had seen. "And they were all amazed and said to one another, 'What is this word? For with authority and power he commands the unclean spirits, and they come out.' And reports of him went out into every place in the surrounding region" (Lk 4:36-37).

As Jesus' language and logic were striking and shocking, so too was his power, for it was unlike any the world had ever known. Jesus lived in a time and place rife with revolutionary movements. His people were oppressed — captives, really, to the Roman rule. Many sought ways to either evade that rule or to challenge it. The Essenes went into the desert; the Zealots advocated revolution.[12] All were looking for someone to restore their fortunes; the Messiah who would be king as David had been. Jesus neither fled to the desert nor advocated armed revolution. He refused to be the king that the people wanted.

Jesus abjured the type of power which was operative in his world and introduced a totally new type. The narrative of the temptation in the desert (Mt 4:1-11 and par.) makes this clear. Jesus refused to use his power to save himself; he could not be tempted by the offer of all the kingdoms of the world. Yet he was able to do things that no one else could do. He healed the sick, made lepers clean and bent women straight. Whole towns brought their suffering to him, and "he laid his hands on every one of them and healed them" (Lk 4:40). He was able to drive out demons, and even the wind and the sea obeyed him. He provided banquets from remnants and gave life to the dead.

This power, which astonished so many and frightened others, was a radical departure from that of his contemporaries. It was not domination or control, but mercy and freedom. The power that went out from Jesus saved people and enabled them. The lame could leap, the blind could see, the deaf could hear. The ostracized and unclean could belong again to the community. The menstruating woman could return home in peace,the mother-in-law could rise and serve, the child thought dead could be fed and regain her strength.

While Jesus' miracles show us unparalleled power, his greatest power was less visible. He had the power to forgive sin. The synoptic gospels all recount the story of the paralytic who was lowered through the roof by his friends (Mk 2:1-12; Mt 9:1-8; Lk 5:17-26). Jesus, touched by the faith of these friends, tells the paralytic that his sins are forgiven. The onlookers are shocked, and well they should be, for they recognize that Jesus has just invoked a power which no human being had. "Blasphemy," they say, "only God can forgive sin!" In response, Jesus tells the paralytic to rise up and walk. He does so in order to show that he can indeed forgive sin. Jesus, as revelation of God, releases the life-giving energy of the kingdom and shows that this energy not only heals and releases, but that it ultimately saves.

There was controversy over Jesus' power, and many questioned the source of his authority. Some who witnessed his miraculous actions asked questions because they knew him as "the carpenter's son" (Mt 13:55), and so thought they knew where he came from. Others challenged his authority directly, saying that it came from the devil (Lk 11:14-20; Mt 12:22-28; Mk 3:22-26). Still others tried to question him directly and received only another question in reply (Mk 11:27-33; Mt 21:23-27; Lk 20:1-8). To those who believed, who knew themselves healed, the source of his power was clear. These praised God for what they witnessed in Jesus.

Jesus not only reveals the power of God, he shows us how that power functions in the world and reminds us again of the paradoxical nature of the kingdom. Although many recognized and sought after the power which Jesus possessed, even those closest to him did not really understand it. They continued to expect that Jesus would lay claim to social power and would reign as king who dominated others. The synoptics record what was probably a frequent topic of discussion: who would be most prominent when Jesus came into his kingdom (Mk 10:35-45; Mt 20:20-28; Lk 22:24-27)? Jesus' response to such talk points out two types of power: that which "lords" it over people and exercises great authority over them, and that in which the greatest must be servant and the first must be slave. The latter description of power is surely illogical and nonsensical in the "real" world; no one really expects to achieve great things by taking the back seat, by being a servant. And yet that, it seems, is how God's power is released. Those who come last are really first, the true disciple is the one who washes another's feet as servants do. Eventually, the follower of Jesus may well be called upon to give up her/his life for others. "The Son of man came not to be served but to serve, and to give his life as a ransom for many" (Mt 20:28).

To those who believed in him Jesus not only taught about power, he also shared it. When the disciples are called they are also sent, and Jesus gives them authority over unclean spirits and over illness. He sends them forth to proclaim the good news and to heal (Mk 6:7; Mt 10:1; Lk 9:1). Jesus apparently did not need to cling to his power (cf. Phil 2:5-11), he did not guard it jealously as that which only he could exercise. The Johannine gospel stresses this point when it tells of a Jesus who declares that his disciples will do even greater works than he has done (Jn 14:12). He seemed to know that God's unlimited power was meant to be given away. He rejoiced when his disciples were successful (Lk 10:17-20), and yet reminded them that they should not glory in their possession of power but in belonging to the kingdom.

The paradox of power is ultimately the paradox of the cross. Jesus, revelation of God, bearer of the kingdom, healer, life-giver, hangs before the world in utter vulnerability and utter desolation. He dies, and in his death life is born anew. One of the most striking and poignant aspects of the synoptic passion narratives is the vulnerability of Jesus. He knows what is about to happen to him, he anguishes over it, and yet he does nothing to protect himself from it. He will not even protect himself from his enemy, the one who has betrayed him. His disciples want to fight with those who would take him, but he will not allow it. He is not violent and will not use violence to save himself. Jesus is not a mighty warrior who meets defeat at the end of a glorious battle. He is one whom a friend can kiss and thus betray.

Jesus dies, and in his death life is born anew. God's power triumphs, and all who would see know now that life wins, that life, not death, is humankind's destiny. The end of Matthew's gospel says that "All authority in heaven and on earth" has been given to Jesus (28:18). Luke tells of Jesus' gift of the promise of God and of the power from on high which will clothe the disciples (Lk 24:49). John talks of Jesus' promise of the Spirit who will teach the disciples all things and will enable them to remember all that he has said (Jn 14:25-26). Jesus' power (Spirit) remains with the disciples, enabling them to continue the proclamation, encouraging them in struggle, giving them hope and wisdom and mission. The kingdom, the strange and gracious kingdom inaugurated by Jesus, awaits full revelation. The power of this kingdom is still overpowered by conventional power of domination and control. For the believer, however, true power lies not in winning or dominating or overcoming. True power is gift and grace; it is life in the midst of death.

Nuclear power, culmination of all power in a patriarchal world, is one which thrives on fear, dominates, controls, and destroys. It is power which shudders at the thought of vulnerability and is based on the capacity to do violence. Emerging feminist power energizes, works best in collaboration, does not fear vulnerability, seeks to enable rather than dominate. If allowed to flourish, it may save the planet. The fulness of power revealed in the life, death, and resurrection of Jesus is radical reversal. Not domination but service; not protection but risk; not hoarded but extravagantly given away. This power heals, gives life, frees from demons, endures, and, most importantly, believes.

Reflection upon the power of Jesus is vitally important for all who would work for peace. Such reflection consistently challenges us to look at our own ways of using and misusing power. More importantly, however, to reflect on the power of God enfleshed in the crucified one gives us hope and encouragement in dark moments even as it reminds us that true power springs forth when the gospel is proclaimed. "For I am not ashamed of the gospel: it is the power of God for salvation" (Rom 1:16).

Relationship in the Kingdom

Although there are moments in the gospel when we are told that Jesus went off by himself to pray, the general sense one has is that of crowds. Crowds followed Jesus, they came to the shores of lakes, gathered outside of houses, sat on hillsides and listened to him, met him as he entered Jerusalem, lined the route of his way of the cross. The presence of Jesus brought people together. Further, this presence brought the most unlikely people together. Sinners and scribes, Pharisees and publicans, tax collectors and fishermen, women and men, Samaritan and Jew — all found themselves joined in amazement and consternation at this one who had appeared among them.

One of the most striking characteristics of the early Christians was their immediate formation into communities. They prayed together, shared their goods in common, broke bread in each other's houses. Fundamental to the preaching of the early church is the centrality of unity among the believers. Staying together is a natural instinct for groups which are new, out of the mainstream, and unaccepted by others; but the intense communities of the New Testament did not arise from natural instinct alone. They were formed in a faith which believed that the Savior was still with them and that life now was meant to be lived together, for "you are all one in Christ Jesus" (Gal 3:28). Understanding themselves as the new people of God, these gatherings of unlikely persons witness to what is essential in the reign of God: union of persons in loving relationship with

God and with each other. The peaceful community grounded in
God's justice envisioned and demanded in the Hebrew scriptures becomes real among those who live in Jesus' Spirit.

The ministry of Jesus as reconciler, which caused such controversy, is firmly grasped in the power of Pentecost. Endemic
to reconciliation is relationship. Each person, particularly the
devalued, is cherished and valued in God's reign; no person is to
remain alone. All are called to relationship, often with those
they would not ordinarily choose. And these relationships are
not to be abstract, theoretical ones but concrete, caring, flesh
and blood sharing of life. There is no room for isolated individualism in the reign of God. The author of John's gospel says
this most dramatically when, in the beautiful and poignant account of the Last Supper, Jesus calls those with him his
"friends" and gives them only one command. "This is my commandment, that you love one another as I have loved you" (Jn
15:12,17).

If we have questions as to whether the kingdom has fully
arrived, we need only to reflect upon the difficulty all of us have
had with this commandment. We know neither what it means
nor how to obey it. I suspect that at least part of our difficulty
comes from our forgetfulness. We tend to forget that the demands of the gospel are indeed heart-stopping at times, and that
these demands are concerned primarily with relationships
rather than with laws or ascetical practice. We also forget
another fundamental message of Jesus' proclamation: that of
forgiveness.

Although most of us pray each day that God will forgive us
our sins, "as we forgive others'," we tend to overlook both the
hope and the challenge contained in this phrase. Jesus proclaimed that in him God had forgiven sin. We have seen that this
claim provoked controversy and charges of blasphemy. His
further claim that forgiving each other is related to God's forgiveness of us (Mt 6:14-15) appears to have been no less difficult
to accept. Yet it could not be ignored and so found its way into

gospel memory (cf. Mk 11:25-26). That it caused difficulty is evidenced in Peter's (everyone's) question: "Lord, how often shall my brother (sister) sin against me, and I forgive?" (Mt 18:21-22). Peter suggests seven times, that is a full number of times (seven, in biblical symbolism signifies fullness). Jesus responds, "seventy times seven." His demand goes beyond any "reasonable" calculation.

Forgiveness of sin, province of God alone, is of the essence of the good news. Salvation is forgiveness and reconciliation. It is wholeness and union. God's activity with humankind is mirrored in the activity of the people. As God is merciful, so too are God's people (Lk 6:36). This is not to say that God's people become miniature gods. Rather, the experience of God's undeserved mercy and forgiveness enables one to be merciful, to forgive in turn. Grace increases grace, love begets love.

Even more striking than forgiveness, but closely related to it, is the gospel call to love one's enemies. Both Matthew and Luke recount this saying, and both place it in significant contexts. In Matthew it appears at the end of a series of antitheses within the Sermon on the Mount where Matthew shows that Jesus' teaching is the fulfillment of the law. "You have heard that it was said, 'You shall love your neighbor and hate your enemy.' But I say to you, 'Love your enemies' " (Mt 5:43-44). In Luke, the saying is the first in Jesus' Sermon on the Plain. "But I say to you that hear, 'Love your enemies, do good to those who hate you, bless those who curse you, pray for those who abuse you' " (Lk 6:26-28). This teaching, "at the heart of his message,"[13] makes clear that the experience of God's love transforms even as it enlivens, and that it transforms within the exigencies of daily life.

Love of enemies is neither abstract nor passive. The "enemies" are real,[14] as is the love. Such love blesses, prays for, does good to, does not seek vengeance. This love actively engages the other in order to heal, to make peace; it is relational, springing from God's infinite love and flowing even to those who hate and persecute.

Relationship, then, is fundamental to Jesus' message and his mission. As reconciler he unites God and humankind. As proclaimer of the good news he draws people together in love and forgiveness. He commands his disciples to love one another and calls them to love of enemies. In a nation which prizes individualism and a culture which equates maturity with individuation, the call to caring community is hard to hear. Forgiveness and love of enemies is scandalous and often viewed as disloyal. All of the cries of the evils of the Soviets and of our need to be able to destroy them are confounded in the call of Jesus. For many, this is nonsense. But, as we have seen, the logic of the kingdom is other than our logic.

Feminist studies, which assert the primacy of relationship within feminine experience, offer a glimpse of the possibility for a transformed world. For believers, that glimpse takes on defined shape in the proclamation; it becomes not only possibility but call. It is the believer's vocation to work to that transformation in *this* world. "Peacemaking is not an optional commitment." It is a scandalous, awesome requirement, possible only in the energizing, empowering experience of the unrelenting mercy of the gracious God.

We live in a time and on a planet overshadowed by terror. Our time may be the last time for humankind. Our planet may cease to exist. We have become used to the terror; we are comfortable with the patterns and theories and name-calling which perpetuate it. We pretend that it is not there; we act as if division and hatred and violence are normal in the course of human life.

Yet, we live in a time and on a planet which are graced with God's presence and God's word. When we approach that word with a listening heart we are stunned by its beauty, by the gracious good news it speaks. God's word, the wondrous, baffling story of a God who chooses and loves and forgives, tells us that our destiny as human beings is peace. This is the will of God for us. There can be no question of that. The Creator cherishes us and our planet. God calls creation to glory, not to misery. There is hope, then, and an easing of the terror in the mercy of the word.

But the hope and the easing are always accompanied by the cry to repent. Ours is a God who does not dominate or control through repression. Ours is a God who invites. It is easy to ignore this God or to disfigure divinity among us. Peace is our destiny. Because our God calls us to peace, because the inviting God invites us to peace, we live now in the light and the urgency of that peace. We wait, but we cannot wait passively or helplessly. We must wait courageously and with risk. Our waiting is that of peacemaking.

The life and mission of Jesus tell us that the reign of God and the fullness of *shalom* have entered human existence. They tell us that *shalom* is available to us, that peace is truly possible. In Jesus and in the memories of the communities who were near him we find the promise and the paradigm of peacemaking. The paradigm is one of conversion to paradox. The gospel calls us to believe the unbelievable, to love the unlovable, to disregard what is "important," to profoundly mistrust our own powers and yet do the impossible.

God's word calls us to a change of heart and the transformation of the world. It tells us that our lives are to be ones of service and compassion, that our hearts are to be filled with forgiveness and courage. It also tells us that we are responsible. Ours is not a faith which resides in the individual but in the people. The disciple is one who not only believes and so is saved, but one who does God's word. The disciple, then, must heal the world, an impossible task were it not for the empowering gift of the Spirit.

We have looked briefly at the facts of the nuclear age, at the terrible costs of nuclear weapons, at the patriarchal ethos which allows terror to thrive and leads us to destruction, at the alternatives to war suggested in revaluing feminine characteristics, at the paradoxical transformation present and yet future in God's word. We look into the mirror of who we are and who we are called to be. There is hope in that mirror and life, even as there is grief and shame. Perhaps if we look deeply enough into that mirror we shall ultimately glimpse the presence of God, at least the hem of the garment. And then we shall know peace.

6
'WHERE IS GOD NOW?'

The word of God provides hope and urgency to one's quest for peace in our world. This word is a gift of never-ending richness whose mystery can never be fully known. It amazes and enlivens us, even as it convicts us in our failure to heed it. Often, however, God's word remains outside of us as object of reflection or as text for study. Even when that word becomes part of us and lives in our hearts, it often appears to have no impact in the larger world. The arms race escalates, violence increases, work for peace falters and appears to fail. Nuclear terror is not diminished, creation is no safer, humankind's future is in doubt. In the midst of the struggle, in the heart of nuclear terror, would-be peacemakers are left with a question. Where is God in all of this?

This question is one which all persons ask in one way or another at many and varying times in their lives. It is symptom of our creatureliness and echo of the deepest longing of our being. How we answer it leads us to despair or exultation. Perhaps the most poignant posing of the question is to be found in Elie Wiesel's account of his experiences in a German concentration camp.[1] Taken to Auschwitz (and later Buchenwald) while still a boy, Wiesel witnessed the deaths of his mother, sister, and father. His mother and little sister perished in the infamous ovens; his father died a few days before the liberation of Buchenwald.

A very religious child, Wiesel recounts his struggle to believe in God in the face of the anguish of God's people. At one
point in his account, he tells of the death of a young boy, one who
"had the face of a sad angel."[2] This child was hanged along with
two adults. All prisoners in the camp were assembled to witness
the execution, all were forced to march past the hanging bodies.
The two adults died quickly, but the child "being so light," took
longer to die.

> For more than half an hour he stayed there,
> struggling between life and death, dying in slow
> agony under our eyes. And we had to look him full in
> the face. He was still alive when I passed in front of
> him. His tongue was still red, his eyes not yet glazed.

Wiesel writes that he heard a voice behind him ask, "Where
is God now?" He heard a voice within himself answer: "Where is
He? Here He is — He is hanging here on this gallows. . . ."[3]
Elie Wiesel's answer is filled with anguish and bespeaks the loss
of faith which he experienced at that time. Few human beings
will ask this question from the depths of incomprehensible suffering as did that man in the face of the slow, agonizing death of
the sad-faced angel and of his race. Yet all human beings who
recognize that all is not right with our world and who nonetheless believe in a creator who cares for creation, eventually ask
where God is, and eventually must give their answer.

Some will say that God is nowhere, that God does not exist
or, if existing, has abandoned us to the misery we have created.
Others will say that God is in the heavens, waiting to either
punish us or avenge us. The presence, the very existence of this
God is a threat. If God will punish us for the situation of the
world, a situation for which no one person is solely responsible,
then God is an intransigent ogre who looms over our existence
and makes us afraid. If God will avenge us, even though we
share responsibility for the world situation, then God is either
blind to reality or quixotic in judgment. The God who waits

beyond creation to punish is threat to all of us. The God who will avenge us is threat to all whom we judge to be our enemies.

Still others answer that God is the one who will come to rescue us. This God will protect creation and not allow it to be destroyed by nuclear annihilation. But what then of our freedom as human beings? If we are honest, we must acknowledge that it is human beings who have created nuclear weapons and it will be through human choice, error or negligence that they will be used. The nuclear holocaust will result from human decision, even if all holocaust is inhuman and most humans suffer only the consequences of the decisions of a few.

None of these answers is adequate; none is worthy of either God or humankind. God is reduced to tyrant or prop. God's presence is far away from us, and we are left here alone, frightened, deluded. For many, and certainly for me, Elie Wiesel's answer is the only meaningful one, although perhaps not in exactly the same way Wiesel intended it to be.

God *is* on the gallows, but God is neither dying there nor rescuing the "sad-faced angel" from death. God is present in the very anguish of that terrible scene. The Judaic tradition knows of a God who liberates by going with the people, who comforts and consoles a suffering Israel, who strengthens the weary, who cries out that it is impossible to give up the beloved. "How can I give you up, O Ephraim! How can I hand you over, O Israel!" (Hos 11:8)

Christians profess to believe in the incarnation. God has *really* entered into human existence in the person of Jesus Christ. If this mystery means anything at all, it means that the divine has chosen to share in the human experience. Redemption happens within human life, not outside of it. Experience is revelatory, it is where God is. It is essential, then, to ponder our experience, to hold it up before our inner eyes in order to see there the presence of God. Our joys and our hopes, the love of family, the tenderness of friends, the forgiveness of those we have wronged, the inspiration of great women and men, the wonder of beauty, the mystery of a silent, star-filled night: all of these show us grace; they are glimpses of the kingdom of God. In their goodness, they move our hearts and make us long for the fullness of grace. Our sorrows and our failures, rejection that we have known, injury that we do, misery which we allow, losses that we carry, our guilt and our remorse: these, too, show us grace, the dark side of grace where we know that the kingdom is not present. When we say, "This is *not* what it is like in the kingdom," we have begun to recognize the kingdom in its absence.

Reflection on experience, the beginning point of all theology according to Dorothee Soelle,[4] leads us to recognize where God is and how God is among us in this world at this time. Meditation upon the word, and reflection on our life experiences are both essential to our lives as Chrisians and as peacemakers. But even these are often not enough to sustain us — peacefully — in the midst of relentlessly growing nuclear terror.

Karl Rahner wrote that "the Christian of the future will be a mystic or he or she will not exist at all."[5] This is eminently true for the peacemaker. What is demanded is mysticism. Soelle defines mysticism as ". . . a perception of God through experience. This means an awareness of God gained not through books, not through the authority of religious teaching, not through the so-called priestly office but through the life experiences of human beings, experiences that are articulated and reflected upon in religious language but that first come to people in what they encounter in life, independent of the church's institutions."[6] Mysticism means that we encounter God, not just writings, theories, meditations about God, but the divine itself. If we would know the meaning of peace, we must know the God of peace.

All classical mysticism speaks of the dark night of the soul, the anguishing experience of nothingness and helplessness when one knows only the absence of God.[7] It is at this moment and in this weakness that the gracious God embraces us. When all of our attempts and plans and schemes, when even our prayer fails us, then God awaits us. When we can do nothing, God does everything.

Nuclear terror is the dark night of our world. It reduces us to helplessness, it fills us with dread, and we cannot escape it. Peacemaking is a process which begins with learning facts, horrible facts and even more horrible realities hidden behind the numbers and strategies and speeches. One then becomes convinced that "something must be done," and resolves to work for peace. For most of us that means speaking out, rallying, writing letters, supporting peace organizations. Most of us have become quite sophisticated in all of this and can quote numbers, contact the networks, organize the demonstrations. We're capable of bringing hundreds of thousands of people together to march for peace, to join hands for peace, to pray for peace. We write highly publicized Pastoral letters and brilliant books . . . and yet not one single nuclear bomb is dismantled, and the President of the United States declares that our nation will begin to disregard Salt II. We feel helpless and futile, acutely so as citizens of a country which prides itself on its proven ability to accomplish anything and everything in the shortest of times. Where is God now?

Here is God; in the heart of the terror. Only when we allow ourselves to dwell in that terror, to own it, to feel it, only then will we truly become peacemakers. Only then shall we be able to answer that question. If we learn to truly see the earth, to savor its beauty, to know it is our home and our haven, we will find ourselves shaken by our love for her and stunned by our grief at the prospect of her destruction. If we begin to see people in their wonder, to dream for futures for all persons, to hope for all who dwell with us on earth, we will also begin to grieve for what we do to each other. We will mourn our violence and our premature death. If we know that forgiveness and reconciliation are the core of peace; we will writhe with the pain of our own smallness, bitterness, enmity. And, finally, if we believe that we are to love our enemies, we can only fall silent before such a demand.

The peacemaker must enter into the dark night of futility and terror, of inadequacy and failure. She/he must rest there in that terrible place and allow the pain therein to enter the very depths of the soul. This is truly an anguishing experience when all we cherish seems to be taken from us, when all our hope seems foolish and all gentleness is violence itself, when all is death and there is no escape or place to hide, for all creation is the sphere of danger. In the midst of this death, if we look and listen, life stirs. God enters to grieve with us, to share our tears, to wrap us in gentleness and hold us in tenderness. This God heals and forgives us, strengthens our bones, stretches our hearts so that we can bear the pain of so much love.

The cacophany of nuclear terror is silenced, and in the great stillness there is the wondrous music of life, the anticipation of dance. The blindness of hatred and violence becomes light-filled vision, and one sees what could be, what is hidden among us. Reconciliation enters our souls; we are one with ourselves again, and joined once more with all that is. We are enabled to embrace again and to continue on in the company of the peaceful God. Knowing blessing, we ourselves become blessing — not because of ourselves but because of the one who surrounds us, who clothes us in grace as all creation is so clothed. And peace enters the world.

The call to peace is call to conversion. It is invitation to learn, to struggle, to work for peace. It is also discovery of who we are and search for alternative ways of being. The call to peace is call to courage to look into our mirror and to repent. Peacemaking leads one into a dark night of terror and to God. It is grace and gift to us in our time.

If we would make peace (and we must make peace), we must continue the struggle against the weapons and against the patriarchal ethos which encourage their creation. If we would make peace (and we must), we must expose the terror among us and know it ourselves. If we would make peace (and we can), we must seek the face of God.

FOOTNOTES

Chapter One

1. National Conference of Catholic Bishops, *The Challenge of Peace: God's Promise and Our Response* (Washington, D.C.: U.S.C.C., 1983), #333.

2. Dorothee Soelle, excerpt from a speech given in Amsterdam, 1981. Reprinted in Cambridge Women's Peace Collective, *My Country is the Whole World* (London: Pandora Press, 1984) p. 231.

3. Ibid.

4. For a more detailed account of this period, consult Alice Kimball Smith, "Manhattan Project: The Atomic Bomb," in Jack Dennis, ed., *Nuclear Almanac: Confronting the Atom in War and Peace* (Reading, Mass.: Addison-Wesley, 1984) pp. 21-42.

5. Kosta Tsipis, "Blast, Heat, and Radiation," *Nuclear Almanac,* pp. 83-97.

6. Herbert F. York and G. Allen Greb, "The Superbomb," *Nuclear Almanac,* pp. 53-65.

7. Ibid., p. 61.

8. Phillip Morrison and Paul Walker, "A Primer of Nuclear War," *Nuclear Almanac,* pp. 129-157, p. 129.

9. York and Greb, "The Superbomb," p. 62.

10. Morrison and Walker, "A Primer," p. 144.

11. Ibid., p. 137.

12. Morrison and Walker place the number of U.S. ICBMs at that time at 300; the Soviet Union had "a couple of dozen," Ibid., p. 144.

13. Ibid., p. 131.

14. Jack Dennis, "Nuclear Weapons Proliferation," *Nuclear Almanac,* pp. 345-365.

15. W.M. Arkin and R.W. Fieldhouse, *Nuclear Battlefields: Global Links in the Arms Race* (Cambridge, Mass.: Ballinger Publishing, 1985).

16. Ibid., pp. 38-39.

17. Morrison and Walker, "Primer," pp. 149-150.

18. Arkin and Fieldhouse, *Nuclear Battlefields,* p. 94.

19. Ibid., pp. 89-91.

20. Arkin and Fieldhouse, in "Appendix A, United States Nuclear Weapons Infrastructure," (*Nuclear Battlefields,* pp. 171-249) give a detailed list of locations and numbers of U.S. weapons and facilities in each of the 50 states and throughout the world. Michigan is found on pp. 194-195.

21. Charles Zimmerman and Jack Dennis, "Nuclear Accidents," *Nuclear Almanac,* pp. 283-300, p. 283.

22. Ibid., p. 285.

23. Two standard references in this field are: Samuel Gladstone and Philip J. Dolan, *The Effects of Nuclear Weapons* (Washington, D.C.: U.S. Government Printing Office, 1977); Office of Technology Assessment, United States Congress, *The Effects of Nuclear War* (Washington, D.C.: U.S. Government Printing Office, 1979).

24. Jonathan Schell, *The Fate of the Earth* (New York: Knopf, 1982). Schell's book originally appeared as a series of three articles in *The New Yorker* magazine (February 1, 8, 15, 1982). The citation is taken from *The New Yorker* (February 1, 1982), p. 48.

25. Cited in Kimball Smith, "Manhattan Project," pp. 38-39.

26. York and Greb, "The Superbomb," p. 54.

27. *The Nuclear Almanac,* pp. 320-321, lists and summarizes all arms control agreements since World War II. See also Bruce Russett, *The Prisoners of Insecurity: Nuclear Deterrence, the Arms Race, and Arms Control* (San Francisco, CA: W.H. Freeman and Company, 1983) pp. 172-173.

28. John Lamperti, "Government and the Atom," *Nuclear Almanac,* pp. 67-81, p. 67.

29. Ed Glennon, "Guide to the Military Budget, Fiscal Year 1985," (Washington, D.C.: SANE Publication, March, 1985).

30. The *Washington Post,* National Weekly Edition, 11 November 1985, p. 15.

31. Glennon, "Guide," p. 2.

32. "Congress Buys Time, OKs Boost in Federal Debt Limit, *Detroit Free Press,* 15 November 1985, p. 4A.

33. Soelle, *My Country,* p. 231.

Chapter Two

1. *Our Youth Speak* (Detroit: Pax Christi, 1983), foreword.

2. San Francisco: W.H. Freeman, 1983.

3. Ibid., p. 53.

4. Harold Willens, "The Trimtab Factor," *The Defense Monitor* 12 (Special Issue, 1983): 2.

5. Russett, *Prisoners,* p. 49.

6. Seymour Melman, "Looting the Means of Production," *New York Times,* 26 July 1981, sec. 4, pp. 21-22.

7. Ibid.

8. Russett, *Prisoners,* p. 51.

9. Seymour Melman, "Butter That's Traded Off for Guns," *New York Times,* 22 April 1985, p. 23.

10. Ibid.

11. Cited in Russett, *Prisoners,* p. 48.

12. Ibid.

13. Joanna Rogers Macy, *Despair and Personal Power in the Nuclear Age* (Philadelphia: New Society Publishers, 1983), p. xvi.

14. Robert J. Lifton, *The Broken Connection* (New York: Simon and Schuster, 1979), pp. 4-5.

15. Ibid., p. 363.

16. Robert J. Lifton, Richard Falk, *Indefensible Weapons: The Political and Psychological Case Against Nuclearism* (New York: Basic Books, 1982), p. 49. Carey's study is referred to in both *Indefensible Weapons* and *The Broken Connection.*

17. Lifton, Falk, *Weapons,* p. 50.

18. Lifton, *Broken Connection,* p. 364.

19. Tim O'Brien, *The Nuclear Age* (New York: Knopf, 1985).

20. Lifton, *Broken Connection,* p. 365.

21. Ibid.

22. William J. Broad, *Star Warriors: A Penetrating Look into the Lives of the Young Scientists Behind our Space Age Weaponry,* (New York: Simon and Schuster, 1985).

23. Ibid., p. 130.

24. Lifton and Falk, *Indefensible Weapons,* p. 82.

25. Ibid., p. ix.

26. Broad, *Warriors,* p. 65.

27. Jim Douglass, "Tracking the White Train," *Sojourners* 13 (February, 1984): 12-16, p. 16.

28. Lifton, *Broken Connection,* p. 339.

Chapter Three

1. Robert Benne and Philip Hefner, *Defining America: A Christian Critique of the American Dream* (Philadelphia: Fortress Press, 1974), pp. 1-16.

2. Ibid., pp. 32-55.

3. Amos N. Wilder, *Early Christian Rhetoric: The Language of the Gospel* (Cambridge: Harvard University Press, 1971), p. 5.

4. Morrison and Walker, "Primer," *Nuclear Almanac,* p. 131.

5. Frank Greve, "Star Wars: A Bolt from the Blue,"*Detroit Free Press,* 17 November 1985, pp. 1A, 18-19A.

6. Mark Gerzon, *A Choice of Heroes: The Changing Face of American Manhood* (Boston: Houghton Mifflin, 1982, p. 41).

7. Lifton, *Broken Connection,* p. 362.

8. Ira Chernus, "War and Myth: 'The Show Must Go On,'" *Journal of the American Academy of Religion* 53 (September, 1985): 449.

9. Robert Scheer, *With Enough Shovels: Reagan, Bush, and Nuclear War* (New York: Random House, 1982).

10. Ibid., p. 18.

11. Ibid., p. 24.

12. Ibid., p. 22.

13. FEMA report, March 31, 1981. Cited in Scheer, *Shovels, p. 110.*

14. Ibid., p. 113.

15. Broad, *Warriors,* p. 105.

16. Ibid., p. 85.

17. Ibid., p. 48.

18. Ibid., p. 105.

19. Ibid., p. 117.

20. Ibid., p. 220.

21. Robert J. Lifton, *Home from the War: Vietnam Veterans: Neither Victims nor Executioners* (New York: Basic Books, 1973), p. 219.

22. Ibid., p. 121.

23. Gerzon, *Heroes,* p. 3.

24. Ibid. p. 171.

25. Macy, *Despair,* p. 13.

26. Gerzon, *Heroes,* p. 90.

27. Cited in Sheer, *Shovels,* pp. 168-172.

28. *The Challenge of Peace,* #132.

29. For an extended presentation of the world view which has dominated western culture for centuries, see Fritjof Capra, *The Turning Point: Science, Society, and the Rising Culture* (Toronto: Bantam, 1982).

30. *Webster's New Twentieth Century Dictionary,* unabridged 2d ed. (1975), s.v. "power."

31. Rollo May, *Power and Innocence: A Search for the Sources of Violence* (New York: W.W. Norton, 1972), p. 99, pp. 105-112.

32. Macy, *Despair,* p. 30.

33. Gerzon, *Heroes,* p. 242.

34. Brad Lemley, "James Webb's New Fields of Fire," *Washington Post,* National Weekly Edition, 23 December 1985, pp. 9-10.

35. Sam Keen, *Faces of the Enemy: Reflections of the Hostile Imagination* (San Francisco: Harper & Row, 1986), p. 129. One must question, however, Keen's reference to women enjoying the "luxury of innocence." Women are profoundly affected by men's ways of "becoming a man." They know very little luxury.

36. Gerzon, *Heroes,* p. 31.

37. Keen, *Faces,* p. 131.

Chapter Four

1. John Simpson and Jana Bennett, *The Disappeared and the Mothers of the Plaza* (New York: St. Martin's Press, 1985), p. 16.

2. Ibid., p. 18.

3. Isabel Allende, *The House of the Spirits,* trans. Magda Bogin (New York: Knopf, 1985), pp. 364-365.

4. "A conversation begins / with a lie. And each / speaker of the so-called common language feels / the ice-floe split, the drift apart / . . ." Adrienne Rich, "Cartographies of Silence," *The Dream of a Common Language: Poems 1974-1977* (New York: W.W. Norton, 1978), p. 16.

5. Susan Brownmiller, *Femininity* (New York: Linden Press/Simon and Schuster, 1984).

6. Ibid., p. 121.

7. See Elisabeth Schüssler Fiorenza, *In Memory of Her: A Feminist Theological Reconstruction of Christian Origins* (New York: Crossroad, 1984), and Letty Russell, ed., *Feminist Interpretation of the Bible* (Philadelphia: Westminster Press, 1985). One should also consult issues of the *Journal of Feminist Studies in Religion* for ongoing discussion of feminist critical interpretation.

8. Rosemary Ruether, in *Sexism and God-Talk: Toward a Feminist Theology* (Boston: Beacon Press, 1983), explores some of these ramifications.

9. Mary Daly, "Gyn/Ecology: Spinning New Time/Space," in *The Politics of Women's Spirituality,* ed. Charlene Spretnak (Garden City, NY: Anchor Books, 1982), pp. 207-212, p. 210.

10. Alice Walker, *In Search of Our Mothers' Gardens* (San Diego: Harcourt, Brace, Jovanovich, 1983), xii.

11. Ruether, *Sexism and God-Talk,* pp. 1-11.

12. Judith Plaskow, "The Coming of Lilith," in *Religion and Sexism: Images of Women in the Jewish and Christian Traditions,* ed. Rosemary Ruether (New York: Simon and Schuster, 1974), pp. 341-343.

13. Robin Morgan, *The Anatomy of Freedom* (Garden City, NY: Anchor Books, 1984), p. xiv.

14. Barbara Starrett, "The Metaphors of Power," *Politics of Women's Spirituality,* pp. 185-193, p. 186.

15. Ibid., p. 188.

16. Carol Gilligan, *In a Different Voice: Psychological Theory and Women's Development* (Cambridge: Harvard University Press, 1982).

17. Ibid., p. 26.

18. Ibid.

19. Ibid., p. 30.

20. Olive Schreiner, *Woman and Labour* (London: T.F. Unwin, 1911), quoted in *My Country,* p. 81.

21. Lifton and Falk, *Indefensible Weapons,* p. 112.

22. The story of the ribbon and photographs of many of the banners are contained in: Lark Books Staff and Marianne Philbin, eds., *The Ribbon: A Celebration of Life* (Asheville, NC: Lark Books, 1985). "Poor Old War God Losing Power" was created by Allie Walton, Deerfield, Illinois.

23. Jean Baker Miller, *Toward A New Psychology of Women* (Boston: Beacon Press, 1976), p. 38.

24. Helen Caldicott, *Missile Envy: The Arms Race and Nuclear War* (New York: William Morrow and Company, 1984), p. 321.

25. Macy, *Despair*, pp. 21-30.

26. Marilyn French, *Beyond Power: On Women, Men, and Morals* (New York: Summit Books, 1985).

27. Macy, *Despair*, p. 31.

28. Jean C. Lambert, "An F Factor? The New Testament in Some White Feminist Christian Construction," *Journal of Feminist Studies in Religion* 1 (Fall, 1985): 93-113.

29. Ibid., p. 104.

30. Ibid., p. 112.

31. Baker Miller, *Psychology*, p. 125.

32. Ibid., p. 126.

33. Ibid., p. 83.

34. Gilligan, *Voice*, p. 160.

35. Baker Miller, *Psychology*, p. 86.

36. Gilligan, *Voice*, p. 156.

37. "Individualism lies at the very core of American culture." Robert Bellah et. al., *Habits of the Heart: Individualism and Commitment in American Life* (Berkely, CA: University of California Press, 1985), p. 142.

38. Baker Miller, *Psychology*, p. 88.

39. Gilligan, *Voice*, p. 174.

Chapter Five

1. All biblical citations are from the Revised Standard Version of the Bible.

2. See Carroll Stuhmueller, C.P., "The Prophetic Price for Peace," *Biblical and Theological Reflections on The Challenge of Peace*, eds. John T. Pawlikowski, O.S.M. and Donald Senior, C.P. (Wilmington, Delaware: Michael Glazier, 1984), pp. 31-44. I also wish to acknowledge the valuable insights contained in a paper presented to the Bishops' committee by the professors of both Old and New Testament studies from the Catholic Theological Union, Chicago (Dianne Bergant, C.S.A. et al., "The Use of the Bible in the Second Draft of the Bishops' Pastoral Letter, 'The Challenge of Peace: God's Promise and Our Response'")

3. Gerhard von Rad, *Old Testament Theology*, 2 vols., trans. D.M.G. Stalker (Edinburgh: Oliver and Boyd, 1968), 1:334-347; Bergant et al., "The Use of the Bible."

4. For a particularly rich exposition of the many meanings of *Shalom*, consult Walter Brueggemann, *Living Toward a Vision: Biblical Reflections on Shalom* (Philadelphia: United Church Press, 1982).

5. See Carol Frances Jegen, B.V.M. *Jesus the Peacemaker* (Kansas City, MO: Sheed & Ward, 1986) for an extended study of Jesus as the paradigm of peacemaking, particularly in terms of Jesus' passion.

6. Consult William Klassen, *Love of Enemies: The Way of Peace* (Philadelphia: Fortress Press, 1984), especially pp. 71-109.

7. For what follows see J.D. Crossan, *The Dark Interval: Towards a Theology of Story* (Niles, IL: Argus Communications) and Crossan, *In Parables: the Challenge of the Historical Jesus* (New York: Harper & Row, 1973).

8. Robert W. Funk, *Language, Hermeneutic, and Word of God* (New York: Harper & Row, 1965), p. 212. See further Funk's study of the parable, pp. 199-222.

9. The Gospel of John, latest and most "abstract" of the four gospels, would appear to speak in a philosophical mode when it stresses the pre-existence of the divine Word or the struggle between darkness and light, being in the world or not of the world, etc. It is important to remember that the Johannine gospel is a more developed meditation upon the meaning of the person of Jesus who often speaks in discourses, who mystifies those who would question him, who stresses that which comes "from above." Nonetheless, the pivotal "logic" of the Christ-event remains central: salvation occurs in the midst of suffering and death.

10. Funk, *Language*, pp. 194-195.

11. Crossan, *In Parables*, p. 83.

12. Sean Freyne, *The World of the New Testament*, New Testament Message 2 (Wilmington, Delaware: 1980), pp. 99-122.

13. Donald Senior, C.P., "Jesus' Most Scandalous Teaching," *Biblical and Theological Reflections*, pp. 55-69, p. 61.

14. Ibid.

Chapter Six

1. Elie Wiesel, *Night*, trans. Stella Rodway (New York: Avon Books, 1960).

2. Ibid. p. 75.

3. Ibid.

4. Dorothee Soell, "Mysticism — Liberation — Feminism," *The Strength of the Weak: Toward a Christian Feminist Identity,* trans. Robert and Rita Kimber (Philadelphia: The Westminster Press, 1984), pp. 79-105, p. 91.

5. Karl Rahner, *The Practice of Faith: A Handbook of Contemporary Spirituality* (New York: Crossroad, 1983), p. 22.

6. Soelle, *Strength*, p. 86.

7. See the fine article by Constance Fitzgerald, O.C.D., "Impasse and Dark Night," *Living with Apocalypse,* ed. Tilden H. Edward (San Francisco, Harper & Row, 1984), pp. 93-117.

Home delivery
from
Sheed & Ward

Here's your opportunity to have bestsellers delivered right to you. Our free catalog is filled with the newest titles on spirituality, church in the modern world, women in religion, ministry, small group resources, adult education/scripture, medical ethics videos and Sheed & Ward classics.

Please send me a free Sheed & Ward catalog for home delivery.

NAME _____

ADDRESS _____

CITY _____ STATE/ZIP _____

If you have friends who would like to order books at home, we'll send them a catalog to —

NAME _____

ADDRESS _____

CITY _____ STATE/ZIP _____

NAME _____

ADDRESS_____

CITY _____ STATE/ZIP _____